IT'S ODD, THE THINGS ONE REMEMBERS

NINA ANN SMITH

◆ FriesenPress

Suite 300 - 990 Fort St
Victoria, BC, V8V 3K2
Canada

www.friesenpress.com

Copyright © 2020 by Nina Ann Smith
First Edition — 2020

All rights reserved.

No part of this publication may be reproduced in any form, or by any means, electronic or mechanical, including photocopying, recording, or any information browsing, storage, or retrieval system, without permission in writing from FriesenPress.

ISBN
978-1-5255-6736-0 (Hardcover)
978-1-5255-6737-7 (Paperback)
978-1-5255-6738-4 (eBook)

1. BIOGRAPHY & AUTOBIOGRAPHY, PERSONAL MEMOIRS

Distributed to the trade by The Ingram Book Company

TO
VERNON AND JOHNNIE
AND
MARY AND MICHAEL

CONTENTS

FOREWORD vii
PART I – EAST OF THE ATLANTIC 1
   Chapter 1 – Kent and Yorkshire 3
   Chapter 2 – Hertfordshire & Surrey 15
   Chapter 3 – The Rest of England – W.A.A.F 33
   Chapter 4 – Worcestershire and London 61
PART II – WEST OF THE ATLANTIC 85
   Chapter 5 – Quebec and Ontario 87
   Chapter 6 – Virginia and Mexico 109
   Chapter 7 – Ottawa again. Growing Up and Away 119
   Chapter 8 – Richmond and Mexico 127
   Chapter 9 – Home to Roost 139
   Chapter 10 – The Challenging Years 151
   Chapter 11 – Afterwards 167
EPILOGUE 185
NAMES AND DATES 187
ACKNOWLEDGEMENTS 189

FOREWORD

Recently I read a book whose dedication was "To the Vanishing Generation". I am one of that generation – the one whose youth and maturing years were shaped indelibly by the second world war of the twentieth century, and whose adulthood has been spent in constant thankfulness that there has not been – will not be? – a third such war.

Vanishing we certainly are, and thus are tumbling over ourselves to record our memories. Indeed, I wonder if any more personal accounts are really needed of air battles, of the bombings of cities, of food rationing or the traumas of displacement and evacuation; of the enormous impact which the life of military service made on ordinary young lives?

So I have tried to place that part of my own life, essential though it be, within a wider context of the idyllic childhood which preceded it, and particularly the far more complex and challenging decades which came after the war. My story is largely typical of thousands of women like me, but there are perhaps a few extra angles – darts which fate aimed at me and adventures on which I was led – to justify my critical mother's grudging admission –

"You have had an interesting life!"

And from my father:

> Promise me that if and when you write, you don't write "for effect".

> What did he mean – for effect? "I mean, how you think it will look to other people, maybe at the expense of factual accuracy or your own true meaning."

So my father's caution led me to watch, edit, condense, and constantly revise my writing.

On the other hand my mother's example in her own thinly disguised fictional autobiography urges me to write "what is true". Not just what is acceptable, careful or inoffensive. "Tell it how it was!"

I can only hope that my story has made successful use of the advice and example of these two exceptional people; my mentors and my unfailing supporters through bad times as well as through good; my adored parents.

PART I – EAST OF THE ATLANTIC

CHAPTER 1
—
KENT AND YORKSHIRE

When you were very small how did you learn to measure – distance, height, direction? I did it this way:

One mile was the *distance* from my house to my friend Mary's house. I walked it often from the age of six onwards; a typical country lane between hedgerows, eastwards along the ridge of our hillside. It was *six miles* by the main road from Sutton Valence to Maidstone, our county town, and the bus took *twenty minutes* in the days when it went directly from one to the other. (Nowadays I hear there are very few buses, and they travel by circuitous ways to economise on routes. "Everyone" of course, goes into Maidstone by car.)

My father was *six feet* tall, so heights in feet and yards were easy. Into adulthood I would find myself, when measuring carpets or room sizes, mentally laying my father out on the floor then multiplying or dividing him as needed. And of course everyone knows that *one inch* is the length of the top half of a grown-up's thumb joint to tip.

For directions? My bedroom window faced *west* – the village chimneys hid most of the sunset but I knew it was there. My parents' bedroom had a bay window facing *south,* and there I would sit in the mornings to wait for the sun to come round from the *east* where, I was told, it had risen. South was the most interesting because beyond our apple orchard directly below that bay window stretched the Weald of Kent and beyond it the English Channel, and France. "On a clear night you can sometimes see the lighthouse flashing at Cap Griz-nez" was often cited as proof of our nearness to the coast of France, though I never saw it myself. But it meant that France was barely *forty miles* away across the Channel, so that was another distance, early absorbed. *North?* Well, north was somewhere up the hill and behind the top road and school – couldn't see north at all.

All these measurements I knew for sure and they were part of the physical framework of my six-year-old life. (As for the flashing lighthouse at Cap Griz-nez, we could not then know that a short ten years later our hillside village would be a vantage point for far more sinister and dramatic flashes in the sky, spelling too often damage and death rather than the life-saving lighthouse. Fighter planes dipping and wheeling, their metal catching the sun, or tracer bullets firing – Heinkel to Hurricane, Messerschmit to Spitfire. Or more distant flashes, accompanied by dull echoing "booms" from anti-aircraft guns, British and German both, aimed from opposite sides of the water at each other's bomber squadrons as well as at the fighters. We had indeed ringside seats, but at performances we would have preferred never to have taken place; aerial contests between a handful of young men from opposite sides in a war that had been thrust upon them – and upon us.)

But back to the village. Peaceful enough in the late 1920s, with the shadow of a previous war slowly receding and no hint, at least to children, of the one to come. Spread along a hillside below the chalky slopes of the North Downs, the two main streets ran parallel to the ridge and were inevitably known as Upper (or Top) and Lower Roads. They were connected at intervals by flights of steps, or steep hilly u-bends – not easy navigation for motor vehicles but very beneficial to pedestrian health. There were in my childhood four pubs, one church, one chapel and five or six shops. Seventy years later all the pubs and the church remain, completely unchanged, but the chapel has become the Art Centre of the local school and there are no shops at all. Not one. Although the population of the village is probably not much changed numerically – 3-4,000? – it has, like many small communities, done so demographically and become a dormitory for town and city workers. They shop at the malls and supermarkets in Maidstone – a mere six miles away, remember? – and either work there or leave their cars at the nearest railway stations three miles away and go to and from London by train.

But the top road is still not the top of the ridge. The land above it rises in shallow tiers of houses and small connecting lanes, then the gardens, the outbuildings and over all at the summit, its clock tower and flag visible for miles from below, the main block of the village's modest claim to fame – Sutton Valence School.

Commonly referred to as "S.V.S.", the main body of the school is a handsome building of red brick, three storeys high with white-framed windows. The centre block contains staff rooms and classrooms, and is bookended by the two senior boarding houses, Westminster and Saint Margaret's. There was much rivalry between the two and anxious debate among the juniors as to which to choose when the time came for them to "graduate up" from Lambe's House, an older building in the lower part of the village.

School! My father's, and later my mother's, employer; the firm backdrop of my days, its existence absorbing all our family's attention and interest; the earliest and strongest influence of my young life and my benchmark for judging my own schools; indeed, many of my future encounters in the world.

In the hierarchy of British Public Schools (private schools in North America) it ranks as a minor establishment. There were in 1930 about 270 boys from age 11 to 17 or 18; my father would say it was just possible to know them all by name. Solid English stock for the most part – the products of a comfortable middle class neither wealthy nor pretentious who wanted for their sons a "good" education. Heavily leaning towards the classical, medium-weight conservative – raising them, hopefully, a notch above the "Grammar School children". In fact though Sutton Valence was founded in 1576 as exactly that; one of three grammar schools established by the Worshipful Company of Clothworkers. The others, also still in existence, are Westminster School and St. Paul's School in London. As the importance of a more universal education was becoming recognised in the 16th and 17th centuries it became the custom of wealthy Merchant Companies to endow such establishments. (On the front of the house where I was born you can see the Clothworkers' Company coat of arms, in the centre of which is a teasel. What is that, I asked when very young, and was told that it was the head of a plant which, when dried was used to separate and card wool before spinning.)

In the 1980s the school, like many other masculine strongholds, succumbed to a feminine invasion – a completely successful move which has improved the tone, character and emphasis at all levels. (I so regret that my father did not live to see this development. Perhaps at first a wry classical comment – "Puellae in sanctum sanctorem veneunt?" (Females, invading our sacred space?) – but I know that he would quickly have accepted and approved of it.) The numbers are now above 400 and – that demographic shift again – the population is vibrantly international.

To this school my father came in 1921 at the age of 22 and remained there for the rest of his life, even beyond retirement. He was an ideal teacher. Patient, thorough, an excellent organiser and above all scrupulously fair. How often in eulogy and recollections from former boys was his fairness extolled above all. Not an intellectual man – he came from a poor family of six children in northern England, and his own education was hard won by scholarship to Lancaster Grammar School and Manchester

IT'S ODD, THE THINGS ONE REMEMBERS

University – but physically strong and energetic, he found his niche and met his own modest goals. My more ambitious mother tried hard to interest him in applying for posts as Headmaster in other schools – to move <u>up and on</u> – but eventually had the wisdom to leave him in peace and turn her abundant talents to expanding her own role in the school and village.

I adored my parents uncritically. Even in hindsight I cannot fault my early childhood in that lovely, peaceful place. We were openly affectionate and close; we worked and played, read and walked, later swam and bicycled, the three of us within a network of friends, school colleagues, and sometimes relatives who came from the north of England – a great distance in those car-less days. A biddable and generally unimaginative child, I must have been easy to raise and I was probably spoilt. Yet when after eight years my brother joined us I felt no possible trace of jealousy; welcomed and worshipped him from the first and took for granted my parents' equal joy in him. Such a gap in our ages meant that, once school claimed him as well as me, our lives did not touch for long periods of time; for a while I was an adult while he a child. (Bill wore his first pair of long trousers, aged just 13, at my wedding in 1945). But once "grown up" we became ever closer, devoted and admiring of each other and remain to this day the dearest of friends. A brother-sister relationship which many envy us.

We were named after our grandparents, maternal and paternal respectively, so I was christened Nina Ann and my brother, Fredric William (in his case with the addition of our father's patronymic Priestley, for which I as a mere female was not considered qualified. This was the 1920s, remember?). A complication was that we were known by our second names, not the first ones, which has caused a lifetime of confusion when dealing with officialdom of any type. No matter; we were Ann and Bill Bentley to all who knew us.

And what of my mother? How do I fairly describe the person who was the first and greatest influence in my life? It will take a while, but the picture must be as complete as I can make it; it is difficult to encapsulate as complex a character as Nell Banks Bentley.

She was beautiful, the loveliest and second youngest of seven sisters (there were also five quite handsome brothers) born to a Yorkshire farmer and his wife in the last two decades of the 19th century. She was intelligent, sensitive, keenly tuned to the beauty of her country world even while taking her share of hard, endless chores in a farm home short of money and high in population. There was little time to give attention to the youngest ones and Nell withheld her own emotions and needs, thinking herself of little account. "Tha's nither use nor ornament" was the accusation most often heard from her preoccupied older siblings, and she has said that she was well into adulthood before she could recognise and acknowledge her own worth and abilities.

Withal her parents were affectionate and supportive where needed, and together with two of her sisters she was able to train as a teacher in London. Thus, self-effacement, strict training in the discipline needed for teaching, and self-control combined to conceal a deeply sensitive nature under a seemingly hard exterior. She could appear formidable even to us, and though we knew the love and devotion were there, it was not until I was middle-aged and read her excellent "autobiographical novel" that I understood how much of herself she kept unrevealed.

She was ambitious, for us and through us; she set high standards and had a clear idea of what she wanted us – including my father! – to do and be. Her teacher training prevented her from readily giving praise (not in those days did teachers write "fabulous!" or "fantastic!" on a piece of work as I recently saw on that of a grandchild). Mama would inspect my appearance before I went out, whether in school uniform or in one of the beautifully sewn outfits which she and a helper made for me (from infancy to the making of my wedding dress). I had to turn, slowly, arms at sides and hands slightly out. If anything was at fault – a belt twisted, a stocking seam awry, hair not tidy – I, not she, must correct it. "You only learn if you do things yourself." If all was well, "You'll do" and a brief smile or hug would dismiss me. How many years later, and at what cost, was I to finally realise that "You'll do" meant she was really very pleased.

IT'S ODD, THE THINGS ONE REMEMBERS

Upper left: my mother, Nell Bentley, nee Banks, the youngest, and most beautiful of 7 daughters and 12 children of a 19th century North Yorkshire farming family. My parents' wedding in 1923. My father Norman Priestly Bentley, in the 1950s, a fair and much-loved school master.

Sutton Valence village.

School - the main building of Sutton Valence School, where my father taught and served as Deputy Headmaster, and around which much of my young life revolved.

IT'S ODD, THE THINGS ONE REMEMBERS

She was so wise, astute and, thanks to her wide reading so informed on the ways of the world even outside her own limited experience, that I really did assume her to be right on most things. She usually was. My father once said to me in later years, when perhaps I had at last begun to question her omnipotence – "You may think I defer to Mummy a lot, but quite honestly it is because she is, simply, just about always right!".

So we three, then four, moved fairly serenely through the fifteen years preceding the second world war. We lived modestly, comfortably, in one of a row of three houses belonging to the school but situated in the village below the hill. They were built as Almshouses in 1888 as replacements for much older ones on the top road; (those buildings in turn had originally been the school's very first classrooms in 1576 and stand today, very little changed.) My father climbed those hillside steps and paths several times a day of his working life – so, indeed did any of us who had need to go all the way to Upper School. From the age of about five I was allowed to make my way up to meet him at the end of morning classes and we would run home hand in hand, down, down again. If I were early I knew I could creep into the classroom very quietly and sit in a corner until the bell rang. This was not exactly encouraged, but neither was it forbidden. As in so many aspects of our upbringing we were expected to know enough to make our own judgements, within the limits of our experience.

Truly we were raised with a most exceptional level of tolerance, guidance and loving support; I realised this quite early on when comparing my home life with others of my peers and I have never, never ceased to appreciate my life's foundation. If my parents were not perfect – their flaws inevitably becoming apparent as we ourselves matured – they were close enough, and any strengths of character that my brother and I possess are directly a result of such a childhood. If this reads as excessive, I can only say that it is true and I know that Bill would agree.

Surrounded by so much academe, what of my own schooling? At age five I joined a few others in Mrs. Smith's dining room – another uphill walk but only one flight of steps this time – to her house behind the King's Head. (Those four pubs make good reference points when navigating around Sutton Valence). I remember the CAT and the MAT and a few sums. I learnt to read quickly and well and loved it, but not maths. After Mrs. Smith's I went into Maidstone – six miles, remember? – to the junior department of the Girls' Grammar School. This entailed a change of buses at the bus station and then a walk of about three blocks. Mummy came with me the first time, after that another child and I were sometimes together, but often I did it alone. I was six years old. Travel by bus, bike, train was just something we did, and from an early age we did it on our own. Public transport was safe, cheap, reliable and frequent; no-one ever doubted for our safety. The bus station Inspector looked out for us sometimes and reminded us to behave on his buses: "remember you are in your school uniform – don't disgrace it!". The same inspector was still there 15 years later when my fiance, awestruck, encountered him while getting on the wrong bus. "You won't get to Sutton Valence that way, sir! you want the No. 12, over there – hurry up now".

I was mildly bullied – teased would be more accurate, but I felt bullied – in junior school. My clothes were "wrong" because my coat was home-tailored, not bought at Blakes', the best department store in town, and my gloves were knitted, not leather. I stood miserably hunched against the playground wall, mute with no answer to the taunts. But I think they cannot have lasted long or been too malicious.

By Form II I had made a dear and lasting friend in Margaret Amos, my Meg, a thin, plain, shy and very clever only child who lived in East Malling, five miles the other side of Maidstone from my home. Again without any apparent trepidation on the part of parents we began to visit each other at weekends or, on long summer evenings, after school, navigating the one-hour bus journeys and transfers without a second thought. Meg's father worked at the East Malling Agricultural Research

IT'S ODD, THE THINGS ONE REMEMBERS

Station, and once when the Duke and Duchess of York visited there Meg was chosen to present the Duchess with a bouquet and a curtsey, and got her photograph in the Kent Messenger. She wore a white dress, long white socks and a big bow on her straight dark hair. She looked pretty, and I was very envious.

(As I write this, that Duchess of York has just died at the age of 101. She became Queen, then Queen Mother, and a few days ago I attended an impressive memorial service for her. She was, after all, an enduring backdrop to the life I am trying to reconstruct.)

Holidays in those years were spent mostly on the North Yorkshire farms of my maternal grandparents and uncles. School summer vacations were long, our expenses after the train fare almost nil, and Daddy's strength and enthusiasm were welcome in the fields. Mama helped with the huge meals and my cousins and I fed chickens, cows, and carried "t'lowance" (the allowance) out to the men in the hot hayfields. Tea, lemonade, scones, biscuits, ham sandwiches, consumed while sitting on the prickly stubble in the shade at the edge of the field, watching the rabbits scurry for hiding from the invasive reaper. We children rode the haywains back to the farmyard and, once the Dutch barn was filled almost to the roof by the sweating older cousins pitchforking the load ever higher, we climbed up and tobogganed down the slippery, sweet smelling pile.

When not needed at the farm we would cycle or bus up Wensleydale to see other branches of the family. Especial to me was my beloved cousin David, two years my senior and as a brother to me. He died at 26 as a result of illnesses contracted while on wartime service with the Durham Light Infantry in India. My sons John David and David Mark, and my grandson David Christopher have helped keep his name for me.

This bucolic, almost 19th century way of life was already coming to an end. Wartime, with increased government support and subsidies, brought some prosperity to farmers and we rejoiced for my hitherto struggling uncles despite the irony of the reason. Two of them with their sons and then grandsons' farm still near Kilburn, but by the end of the 1900s small-holdings had again become unprofitable. The solid stone houses have become first-class Bed and Breakfast establishments, and "The Mouseman" of Kilburn and "the James Herriot country" of the Dales bring many tourists.

In particular a member of the current generation of my mother's family, the Banks, has brought unexpected wide fame to our tiny corner of the North Riding. Tommy Banks, great-grandson of my uncle Thomas, the youngest of those "five quite handsome brothers", has become a highly skilled Master Chef and received the coveted Michelin Star for the world-class cuisine that he offers at The Black Swan, in the small hamlet of Oldstead where I spent those 1920s summers. Together with his parents and brother he has transformed the shabby local pub (known in my childhood as "T'Mucky Duck", where we only ventured if sent to buy cigarettes for aunts and uncles) into one of Britain's best and most well-known restaurants. World travellers come not only for the superb food but to stay overnight in the charming rooms which the family has built beside the pub – or in Rose Cottage around the corner, which was my Banks grandparents' last home, and where I spent many long early childhood summer holidays. Too, the visitors admire the large vegetable garden which the family has created and whence he harvests the bounty for his superb menus.

How bemused – and I hope, how proud – they would be, those resilient forebears who loved and toiled that land before him.

My father was a keen mountain walker and my first visits "abroad" were on walking holidays which he organised for parties of boys from school, in the summer holidays of 1938 and '39 to the Swiss and French Alpine regions. By then, at 14, I was as interested in which boys were going as I was in which places we were to visit. A heady atmosphere for a romantic teen, and it was considered time to distance me from my "fan club" as one master described it, as well as for me to acquire some further education.

CHAPTER 2

HERTFORDSHIRE & SURREY

As always in my parents' eyes "good schooling" was paramount and meant taking pains to find the best they could afford. I sat for scholarship exams at two schools – neither were in the ranks of the fashionable, but had good academic reputations. I did not gain a scholarship to either. It was intimidating to be taken, on two separate occasions, to overnight in completely strange places among scores of curious girls and to take a series of tests in forbidding classrooms. Nevertheless I did well enough for my parents to take a chance and I was enrolled at Berkhamsted School for Girls, about 50 miles north of London. Being mostly a day school, with only about 10% of its 400 pupils being boarders, its fees were lower than some. Even so they, and the cost of books, uniform, train travel and an inevitable list of "extras" each term which infuriated my mother, were a drain on the family finances and probably only affordable at all because my father's working situation had changed for the better.

His school designated the row of three conjoined cottages, of which our home had been on one end, to be converted into a boarding house for twelve boys. My father was to be its Housemaster, and to his modest pride, the building was named "Bentley's House". (However, after he moved up the hill to Westminster and became Second Master of the school, Bentley's was rechristened "Holdgate's House" after a deceased headmaster.)

Bentley House – my childhood home

This change to our house also brought, to her huge pleasure, my mother's designation as House Matron. Not only did my father receive an increase in his salary, but she was also paid a small one OF HER OWN. ("You know Ann for fifteen years I had to ask him for every penny I needed" was often heard when describing her satisfaction at this development.) How very good she was at this job, and how she blossomed, with two young maids to train and to help her, and a "real" household to organise. That was the beginning of a period of quite gracious living in our home, before the shortages of wartime became felt; new paint, new furniture and clothes – more FUN. With Mama, relaxed and confident at last, at its centre.

But to return to Berkhamsted. I began there in the fall of 1938 at age 14 ½, expecting to finish an established curriculum of Matriculation one year and Higher Certificate the next, the equivalent of University Entrance. To my everlasting regret, and with my parents apologetic reluctance, it was decided in 1940 that I must leave school and get some kind of career training before the hazards of war affected even our small lives more seriously – either by closing or evacuating Sutton Valence School, or in the worst case its being bombed. Our village lay in the path of the German raiders and they often emptied the last of their loads around us on their way home from the increasingly heavy attacks on London . Remember those dog-fights over the Weald?

But I did get my Matriculation, with honours in English, French, Latin and History, and in the process I spent quite simply two of the happiest years of my young life. I suppose I quickly fitted in because the routines and disciplines of boarding school life were so familiar to me. Sure there was some homesickness and confusion until the rules were sorted out and friends made, but after a few weeks I felt myself to be a veteran. My letters were long and enthusiastic. My mother liked to tell – though I cannot remember the incident – that at the beginning of the holidays following my second term she found me weeping in my room. On being asked what was wrong, I apparently wailed "I'm schoolsick! Nothing's happening here!".

I lived in a house with about sixteen girls aged from 13 to 18. The three boarding houses were converted private homes; large, solid, ugly buildings about 30 years old across the road from the school buildings (more modern), pool and playing fields. At Loxwood we had our own garden and lawns, large rooms for study and eating and a basement "playroom" and we slept 3 or 4 to a room on the two upper floors; curtained-off cubicles each with a bed, wash stand and dresser. There were maids, a cook (a super cook was Thirza; we chose our own dinner menu on our birthdays); a House Matron and a House Mistress. And this, as I have said, was not a wealthy school; Britain was even yet a land of cheap domestic labour and the women who worked for us would be better paid than if they were in private service.

Loxwood House at Berkhamsted. Loxwood Girls 1938-39; Nina Ann Bentley (NAB) at the centre of the front row.

IT'S ODD, THE THINGS ONE REMEMBERS

The academic staff were without exception female, single and mostly middle-aged. They were known by their initials and surname – I don't remember ever knowing a single Christian name of even my favourites. The headmistress, Miss C.F. MacKenzie – Mac, inevitably and always among ourselves – was a Scot, small, compact, low-voiced and stern, but it was on her administrative and intellectual strengths that the school's then excellent reputation rested and which had attracted my parents to it. She took morning prayers every day of term, presided over Prize Giving, and I think she taught some subjects in the sixth "VI" form, but rarely came into any other classroom. Except for my initial interview, and the receipt of a treasured postcard handwritten by her telling me my Matric. results – with congratulations! - I had no contact with her in my two years. We did not like or dislike her; we respected her; she was simply there.

My housemistress at Loxwood was a 50-ish (how old!), very erect History specialist named Miss Mace. She too had a stern appearance but since we all lived together we got to know her, and in my second year we house monitors met with her often and easily. I remember once on her nightly round of the dorms she was mesmerised by the sight of three or four heads sheathed in hair rollers and nets. "What an awful sight! how can you possibly sleep in those things?" exclaimed she of the severe, straight grey bob. A very knowledgeable, interesting woman; I would have enjoyed her as a contemporary, I think.

In contrast to Miss Mace, our first House Matron was a younger, quite stylish military widow named Mrs. Cairns. She must have been very young when her husband was killed in the last months of WWI; she had two boys at boarding school and was determined to earn enough to keep them there. She seemed rather sad; lonely, no doubt. But she looked after us capably enough and lost no time in taking us new girls in hand to remedy any perceived deficiencies in our clothing and toilette. In my case this involved providing me with brassieres and deodorant – items that appeared, to my mother's consternation, on the end-of-term bill. In my home the former had been considered adult-only wear; young girls wore "liberty bodices", a kind of undervest made of ribbed cotton intended to give some restraint even to developing teens. Deodorant products were considered somewhat sissy extravagances; a daily bath and the liberal use of talcum powder having sufficed until now.

Thus our minds and bodies were cared for and directed. Withal, we also had a great amount of fun. Friendships were close; inevitably as our emotions budded there were passions, "crushes" and rivalries. Some of us were religious, some political – a few were slightly snobbish. In the fading days of Empire British boarding schools were still depositories for the children of colonials who were keeping the Union Jack flying in Africa, India and to a lesser extent in the Far East. Peggy's parents would come "home" from India for Christmas only – they whisked her and her sister off to a hotel, which I thought so luxurious and sophisticated, but the girls hated it and envied us our real homes.

Like the majority of schools in the country ours was based solidly on the tenets of the Church of England. Yet if there were girls of other faiths or, rarely, other colours, they were accepted without fuss; they didn't have to come to church or prayers and no-one made anything of it. Nor did we isolate or remark on others who might appear different; if Charmian were "a bit slow" she was accommodated in the regular classes; if Shareen could not eat certain things, Thirza in the kitchen did her best.

For us "ordinaries" there were morning prayers and Sunday matins at St. Peter's parish church, a typically large and ugly 19th century edifice. We walked there in crocodile, yes we really did, every Sunday at 10.30. Once we were confirmed we were also expected to walk down for 7.30 Communion. This hardship could be softened if one willing person managed to faint, or at least feel faint and have to be escorted home. And there was a good Sunday breakfast to follow.

I did not become particularly religious at this time, though I did find the classes leading to confirmation, and the rite of passage itself, to be moving and interesting, because it was well taught and interpreted by the local vicar. But the <u>words</u>, the litanies and prayers and above all the hymns fed my love of language. I had a reasonable contralto voice and managed to sing in choirs from schooldays on. This grounding in a ritual which I only half believed stayed with me and, though buried for long periods of doubt, rejection and experimentation with alternative religious forms, evolved in my later years into a very personalised, if unorthodox, set of beliefs to live by. I call it a mildly practical Christianity. Though still rejecting the mythological aspects of the Christian church and unable to recite its creed, yet I have drawn strengths from my interpretation of it.

What else did I learn? Much the same as I had begun at Maidstone, but somehow it all came together so much better when we lived and worked and played together; always there was someone available to compare notes or prep (homework), and to share the apprehensions before tests or the jubilation at the end of exams. I continued to play the violin, badly, as I had since the age of 10. It was tactfully suggested that I drop it when the Matriculation year began. We did lots of plays – like singing, I was able to keep up my acting well into adulthood. I learned the game of lacrosse, having previously played only field hockey; I still have in a drawer my bronze medal of the Royal Life Saving Society in swimming. My confidence grew and I made close and lasting friendships.

Two girls came to Loxwood from Belgium and Germany whose arrival and experiences made a great impression on us. By 1938 many European Jewish families were sending their children to British schools. Poor Francoise and Luzie – they were so lost and miserable, with not a word of English and no clear idea as to why they were there. But they learned, adapted, and became among our brightest and dearest.

I have written in detail about this tiny period – two years out of nine decades. I hope this shows what a deep influence those years had; how successful were the principles of "character building" on which generations of fine teachers like Mac and my father set so much store, and built their lives' work.

In my 16th year I was made a House Monitor, took the Matriculation exam as related earlier, and looked forward to a heady final year in the Sixth Form, reaching with my best friends the heights of responsibility and privilege; to becoming those Olympians to whom the "little girls" looked up with awe.

Instead there came an unexpected, very rare visit from an apologetic and worried Daddy. He explained over tea in a town café that I could not after all realise that dream. I was deeply impressed by his showing me a notebook containing, in his minute and orderly handwriting, complete details of our family's financial situation, and how it would be affected if he lost his job or his life. My pride in having this shared with me, and the fact that he thought it – and me! – important enough to come 70 miles across London by bus and train to do so, masked for a while some of my great disappointment. That resurfaced all the more keenly three months later. At the end of a long family summer holiday cycling the Yorkshire dales, brightened by the presence for a while of one of my most treasured school friends, came the date of the beginning of the new school year. But I was not heading back to Berko in my navy coat and skirt, my dark green velour hat with the blue and silver house band around it or my blue and silver house tie. I was not joining Peggy and Anne B. and Daphne and Phyllis in the Sixth. Instead, the next phase of my training had been decided upon and set in motion – a six-month secretarial course. How dreary that sounded! I would like to have been a teacher and my work experiences in later years showed that I would have been a good one. But to train as a teacher meant university, and that had been ruled out. My mother did not consider me university material, my father could not afford the fees, and the uncertain future facing us all returned us to the already-decided; I must train for "something useful" while there was still time.

Once again my parents' knowledge of the network paid off. Mrs. Hoster's Secretarial College was reputed to be one of the two best in the country. However in 1941 it had been evacuated, like so many establishments, away from London to the town of Tunbridge Wells, conveniently for us only 25 miles from Maidstone. Once again I was housed with other young women, this time in a converted mansion much grander than my dear ugly Loxwood. Salons with brocaded wallpapers, extensive grounds, deep large cellars where we spent many nights of broken sleep as the air raids increased.

More good friendships came my way; best of all with Anne Fletcher, who became Anne Wilson, wife of the dashing Glaswegian Naval officer, Ramsey, and who remained unquestionably my dearest and closest ally and confidante. More of Anne and her family later.

Mrs.Hoster's Secretarial College, 1940 – NAB seated at right

These six months from October 1940 to early April 1941 brought changes in our family life, which for the first time became fragmented and inconvenienced by the fringes of the war. My mother, finding that volunteer work with the local branch of the Red Cross insufficient use of her real training, became a supply teacher and agreed to serve in areas of North Yorkshire near to her own relations. This meant establishing a second home for her and my then 8-year-old brother, the closing of my father's boarding house and the creation of a semi-bachelor existence for him. He continued to live in our now half-empty house but took his meals at school. His teaching load, his duties in the Home

Guard and as an Air Raid Warden left him little leisure, but leisure was becoming an elusive luxury for most people.

I was able to hitch a ride home from college on alternate weekends with a commuting neighbour, which gave Daddy and me a few hours of mutual cheering-up and companionship. But not much physical comfort, the biggest problem being, what could we eat? Ration books had to be deposited with whoever was providing one's meals, in my case the college and in his the school, and without rations there was little scope. We scrounged from kind neighbours, and there were always fresh fruit and vegetables in that corner of Kent, the "garden of England".

We were now losing a lot of sleep; nights were being increasingly fragmented by air raids. First the distant ack-ack (anti-aircraft) guns on the Channel coast, then nearer ones on inland airfields. Then the warning sirens, and THEN the most threatening noise of all; the unmistakeable, sinister, throb-throb of the enemy planes coming in – it was only then I remember I was really frightened. We did not expect to be bombed, knowing they had more important targets such as poor London, the docks, or the east Kent ports of Rochester and Chatham, however, bombs were routinely dropped at random on their return to Europe, to lighten their loads and enable them the better to try to dodge our fighters and guns. Although our village was never directly hit, a small bomb was dropped on the playing field some distance behind the Upper School causing great excitement and no damage other than a ruined rugby pitch. But it was that dreadful opening chorus of throbbing engines which tightened the muscles of the heart and spelt true fear.

Apart from these "inconveniences" my secretarial course passed pleasantly enough. The work was well-taught and quite comprehensive; it even included French shorthand as well as the conventional typing, book-keeping, etc, and high marks were required to pass the completed course. My closeness to Anne Fletcher extended to embrace her wonderful parents when she took me to stay with them at Guildford, a short train ride away. Her father was a career RAF officer – " A Wing-Commander!! " – as I heard an awe-struck Bill telling his mates. Anne had an older

IT'S ODD, THE THINGS ONE REMEMBERS

sister and brother; Pamela was living at home waiting for the birth of her first child; her husband and the brother were both in the army in France. Both were wounded at different times, but recovered.

The whole family was very musical and helped me to develop my own half-formed musical tastes and abilities. Mrs. Mary Fletcher and Pamela, her second daughter, played the piano well; Anne the viola, and she and I SANG, always, all over the place; Wingco (our affectionate name for Anne's father the Wing Commander) also had a fine voice. As for brother John, the only time I met him was after the war, and I heard him ask his sister – "I know you have bought me that Brahms record for my birthday; can I have it NOW?". So, the music was there, too, and the connection stretched further when, nearly two years later, I visited the home of John's fiancée in Northumberland on a weekend pass from the WAAF and was first introduced to the works of Gilbert and Sullivan.

After college came the hunt for jobs – the working world at last. Not very onerous, perhaps, for a 17+ year-old still supported by her parents, but I do fondly remember the black two-leather wedge-heeled sandals I bought with my first pay – plus a small pair of blue china vases for mama, to hopefully cancel my selfish purchase.

For a short while I worked in London for a small branch of the Red Cross. Apart from its location, a shabby/genteel house near Hyde Park, and the fact that I disliked the woman who ran it (a snobby, self-important type puffed up beyond her abilities to fill a wartime-created position), I remember little about the work. The interlude is best pin-pointed by an incident described in the following letter of mine which was published in the Toronto Globe & Mail on 12th September, 2001, following the World Trade Center attacks:

> On Sept. 11, 1941, I emerged from the London Underground station nearest to my place of work in London – emerging, I was expecting, into the sunny light of day that I had left behind at home in the country.

Instead, I was at once showered by dust, choked by smoke, picking my way through shattered glass on the sidewalk. Firemen and policemen surrounded me. "Get back, Miss, you can't go there" I was told. And I saw that it was my building that had been partly destroyed, the building I had left only 15 hours before.

I was 17 years old; that was my first paid job.

Of course I felt fear. But I knew my enemy. He had a name, a face, a very clear identity. Twelve months later, I would be in uniform, trying to help down him from the sky whence he was raining such destruction.

The fear I felt Tuesday, 60 years later, as I watched again the dust and smoke and broken glass, the firefighters and the police officers and the dazed people in New York City, was in some ways a worse fear. I do not know my enemy, and I cannot put on a uniform to fight him.

May we all soon know his face.

N. Ann Smith, Ottawa

The redeeming feature of those weeks was that I lived with the Fletchers because the journey by tube and bus to and from Guildford was shorter, easier, and cheaper than from Sutton Valence, where Daddy was still subsisting in very domestically reduced circumstances. I felt a bit, but not very, guilty; I was SO comfortable! – so cossetted and made much of, so absorbed into the family.

It seemed to me in those days and up to the time of Anne and Ramsey's engagement and wedding in August 1942 that Mrs Mary Fletcher made something of a confidante of me. She was, as were so many women of her class, beset and bewildered by the hundred new difficulties and restrictions of running a household. Previously such a ménage as hers would have run itself, with efficient staff and unlimited resources. Now she had to cope with rationed food, reduced and oft-changing help, and unreliable infrequent news of absent family. With great apology she explained to me, soon after my "boarding arrangement" was under way, that my bedlinen would not be laundered after every visit of 2-3 nights, but would be carefully folded, labelled and put in the linen closet until next time. "But of course dear, we will always wash the towels!". (The boarding arrangement my parents had quite rightly insisted on paying for, but against worried protests from Mary who was such a stranger to the crass world of commerce.)

What a darling she was, and how satisfied I was when she and Wingco were finally able to meet my own parents. She died very suddenly in 1955 when she must have been barely 60 years old. Jack was bereft and almost helpless; he lived variously with his children, eventually in a residence until old age and near blindness caught up with him. He and I corresponded regularly. I was "AB" to the family, so with AB and Wingco we signed our letters.

By the autumn of 1941 I had had enough of the pseudo-gentility of the Red Cross office and obtained – I forget exactly how – a "real" job in the typing pool of the Central Electricity Board, the organisation responsible for the creation and maintenance of the power grid throughout the British Isles. A salary! benefits! paid holidays! and I was on the road! Admittedly the young women of the Pool, overseen by a tight-lipped disciplinarian known to us simply as The Clarke, were not very different from the high spirited crowd at college. Even our living arrangements were similar, because the CEB also had evacuated its London offices and was established at Horsley Towers, a large ugly sprawl of a pseudo-castle in Surrey. We slept in odd-shaped tower rooms, washed in vast cast-iron sinks and tubs in cavernous chilly bathrooms, and worked in long wooden huts erected temporarily in the grounds.

BUT – Horsley is only two stops on the railway line from Guildford and the Fletchers' home! Once again my weekends were lightened and brightened by whatever entertainment Anne and I could find. Movies of course – I think I went to the cinema more often during the war than at any other time – the occasional local dances, and visits to London. One could not stay away from brave, battered London; there was the feeling one wanted to share its pain. Even so we could not have guessed how dramatically one of our outings there would end.

In late 1941, with the Battle of Britain effectively over but with heavy raids still occurring, Anne and I and some friends went to see The Dream of Gerontius at Queen's Hall. This was new magic for me; my first exposure to a live performance of a serious musical work. When we came out the All Clear had just sounded after a "warnings-only" – no raid this time. We made our way to Waterloo Station, the dimly lit train, and the walk home through darkened Guildford streets. The biscuits and thermos of tea which always awaited latecomers were joined this time by Anne's mother who, made anxious by the raid warnings, had waited up for us.

In the early hours of the next morning came again a severe bombing of London and Queen's Hall was completely destroyed. Broadcasting House next door, headquarters of the BBC, was badly damaged. Our Dream of Gerontius was the last ever performance in that historical building where many British composers, conductors, orchestras and performers had played and sung.

I soon became established in the routine of office life and the limited but pleasant social scene that grew up around it. Since most of the Board staff and employees were living and working in the same place all week, quite good programs of entertainment were organised; concerts of both live and recorded music, plays, tennis and even, briefly and memorably in mild-wintered England, skating parties on the lake.

But my real interest and attention now turned back to home where our family was made blessedly complete once more by the return of mother and Bill from Yorkshire. The danger of invasion was past and that of air-raids diminished sufficiently for the school to re-open Bentley's House, its twelve boys thus needing their Housemaster and Matron once again.

IT'S ODD, THE THINGS ONE REMEMBERS

Oh, how happy we were! Probably those were the best months we would ever spend all together. Mama was tired after two years of teaching in remote places, lodging in austere northern farmhouses and handling a mixture of suspicious country children and confused evacuees. Not least of her trials, a strong-minded eight-year-old son who had made the most of his position as teacher's boy with no male discipline as back-up . But her energies soon revived, and the household expanded further to include my cousin, Renee Whaley, with her two small children – Mary, a solemn 4-year-old, and 20-month-old Tom. They stayed with us to be near her army husband, Dawson, stationed a mile away at East Sutton Park. Tom was a source of pride to me, being the first of my godchildren. These would eventually be eight in number as friends and relatives laboured under the delusion that I possessed godparental qualities. Did they perhaps think I would marry a rich man and leave them money? Whatever, I took my duties seriously and have had, still have, enormous pleasure from keeping in touch with them all in three different countries, and seeing some of them when I can.

Visiting home, 1940s; after my mother and brother Bill had returned from evacuation to the north.

I was now just over 17, and though my own schooldays were 18 months behind me, many of the S.V.S. boys of the same age were still in the VI form, either marking time until they could enlist at 18, or waiting to decide what to do until they were called up. A group of about six of them, mature enough now to have shed the old awkwardness around "masters' daughters", accepted me easily as one of them when I came back home for the weekend. 20-month-old Tom in his stroller would find himself being whisked around the edge of the cricket field, or the centre of attention by a damp circle of swimmers by the pool. There were "away" matches, cricket or rugger, when we went by bus or train to other schools to cheer our own side.

There was Peter Comrie, head of school – he was to become an Admiral in the Royal Navy. There were the Palmer twins, John and Ronald, who were killed in Sicily and India. There was Robin Burns, a devoted admirer of my father, who lives still in Vancouver and whose daughter is one of my godchildren. There was Andreas Karlebach who came, as Lucie Hahn had come to Berkhamsted, shy and inarticulate from Germany. He became Andrew Carlson, a proud naturalised Englishman; from him also I sometimes receive a telephone call. There was Edward Atienza, my dear Teddy. A pianist, a singer, an actor; small dark and lithe, he became a wise and needed counsellor and intermediary during the next two or three years as the lines of our service lives ran parallel and sometimes crossed. Acting became Edward's profession and I was able to follow his career as later he too came to Canada and worked with the Stratford Company and at the National Arts Centre in Ottawa.

Then there was Theo.

I didn't much like him at first, absorbed as I was in the more obvious glamour of the blond handsome gods of sport and swimming. He was tall, thin and somewhat ungainly – loose-limbed I suppose but I called it "gangly". His nose was short, his chin not strong, yet with thick dark hair and very fine brown eyes the overall impression was of a remarkable head. He was plagued by a stammer in his speech – only later, softening, did I realise what a miserable, paralysing affliction that must be. Spoilt individual that I was I had little patience with his early hesitant attempts at conversation. How did things change? Very gradually, with many ups and downs, advances and withdrawals on both sides, we found common interests and ways of spending short periods of time together as well as with the others.

He was first and foremost an artist, and could be found in the fields or lanes around the village with a sketch book or a book of poems; I, walking with our black Labrador Barney, would stop and look, read or listen. He was at that time much "into" the concept of reincarnation and plied me with books by Joan Grant and others. Like Edward he was a very good actor, and I had admired his recent performance as Abraham Lincoln in a school play – the stammer, over which we all agonised at dress rehearsals, vanquished completely on the final night.

On this occasion I met his mother, Margaret, for the first time. She sat with us and I observed, I thought, a smart and animated lady. Never would I have guessed that within two years I with the rest of her family would be struggling to help her through a strange and chronic depression which left her increasingly vague and disconnected from the practical side of running a household; chain smoking cigarettes, rather untidy of hair and clothes, ("Ann, can you please sew some buttons on Mother's coat?"); sweet and affectionate still but somehow, just somewhere else. Of Theo's father, Major Reginald Hancock – author, respected veterinarian, gifted amateur singer – a wise and charming character – I shall have more to say.

My parents observed these developments with interest – my father with some trepidation. Was it quite proper, and to what extent should he condone his daughter's public appearances with one of his prefects? The test of this acceptance came when Theo asked, with great respect, if he might invite me to tea in his Show (study). Oh, poor Daddy! I don't know which of them showed the greater courage, Theo for asking or Daddy for finally agreeing – but on condition that Mama accompanied me. This was not such a damper as it might seem; Mummy and I enjoyed any new adventure that we did together, and Theo like most of the boys adored the lovely and interesting Ma Bentley. Nevertheless, it was an Occasion. Prefects' Shows were sacred places, small cluttered rooms usually shared by two boys and redolent of socks, ink and burnt toast. Their windows overlooked the lawns and terraces of top school so all comings and goings were clearly visible. I suppose tongues wagged, especially when once later I did go for tea on my own, but there was no criticism, no repercussions; my father's stature among staff and boys was unassailable. I really believe he could do no wrong in that place, to which he gave his energies and skills and support for over forty years.

CHAPTER 3

THE REST OF ENGLAND – W.A.A.F

Following a long, cold, increasingly war-weary winter came the spring of 1942 and a year of still more changes for many of us. In November 1941 the battleship Ark Royal, on which Ramsey Wilson was serving, was torpedoed and sunk with the loss of many sailors. He was not among them, but the experience hastened his and Anne's resolve to marry much earlier than they had originally planned. At very short notice a happy wedding took place and the reception held in the big Guildford garden. My favourite memory, oddly enough, is of Mary Fletcher and me cooking and dressing a huge salmon that the Scots relatives had brought; an otherwise unobtainable luxury at that time. And of Mary, perturbed, asking me if I thought this marriage would endure "despite the difference in their ages"? I thought it a bit too late to express any doubt, and in any case I don't think Ramsey was more than nine years older than Anne. Indeed the marriage endured most strongly, through some cash-strapped years on an Inverness farm, through the arrival of three sons, (Andrew the eldest, one of my godsons, still in touch with me) to a serene retirement and Anne's too-early death soon after they celebrated their Golden Wedding.

Come now to the summer of 1942, the golden, blissful summer of my eighteenth year. Yet there was guilt in being carefree at such a time. The war surrounded us; we mourned the steady procession of losses in all its sectors but especially at sea in those months when the German U-boats took their heaviest toll of North Atlantic convoys; we feared the future even while steadfastly believing in victory; we resolved, above all, to "pull more weight." In my case this translated into a decision I had been leading up to for some months; to leave CEB and join the Womens' Auxiliary Air Force.

Almost ten months before I had begun some fact-finding about the womens' services. My diary of the time states rather primly that "I should do my share – here are my friends dying while I sit comfortably at home". I had strong encouragement from mama, always one to seize new experiences: "if there has to be a war you might as well learn something from it". Very much less enthusiasm from prudent, careful Daddy. Why would a young girl – HIS girl – want to leave a secure job with good prospects for the murky unknown of female barracks life? In this he was unexpectedly supported by the administration at CEB. The Board ranked as a Protected Industry, i.e. employees were deemed to be in essential service and so exempt from call-up. I was given a hard time, and in two or three increasingly unpleasant interviews pressure was put on me to stay. I was made to feel that I was being disloyal, positively unpatriotic! I was intimidated, not accustomed to having to stand my ground, but I did so, with mother's exhortations echoing in my head; made my farewell rounds for the third time in under two years, and went home. Home to my beloved village and family and to

IT'S ODD, THE THINGS ONE REMEMBERS

this strange, compelling new friend, to savour them all to the utmost for the remaining weeks.

Theo had finally left school, having gained a scholarship to Oxford which in the event he could not take up until after the war. He would come for a dance, a movie, always a constant exchange of letters, books, and a growing portfolio of watercolour sketches of the village and places which became significant to us. One or two he gave me, but more were bought by mother who encouraged his talent: "it's time we had some artistic bent in this family". All hang on the walls of my home in Canada to this day.

But there was no question yet of his being family. Our emotional life was choppy, up and down, very much at the mercy of his nervous temperament and my more even, if sentimental one. It soon became a case of "can't live without you, but know I could never live with you". For the time being it had to suffice that we were everything to each other; discussion of the long-term future was avoided because immediate separation loomed.

On 24th August 1942 I received my marching orders. My parents watched me and a handful of other apprehensive Kentish girls board a train for London, there to change stations and head west to a town called Bridgenorth of which I had never heard, in a part of England I had never seen. I was, I suppose, better prepared for this adventure than the others, since the recruiting officer who despatched us from Maidstone summed us up and put me "in charge". Some of them had never been on a train, let alone as far as London.

Indeed it was a huge new world in which we found ourselves. I said in my foreword to these remembrances that I would not dwell in detail on my WAAF years. Not that they were unimportant – they were probably "the making of me" and led me by unexpected turns to the rest of my life. But similar experiences have been extensively written up by others; there was a rash of books around the 50th anniversary of the end of the war in 1995 and one at least could literally have been written by me. My diaries record it all. "The sea of blue uniforms, with non-blue newcomers sprinkled through it"; the barrack blocks, the endless queues to join more queues; vaccinations, drills, spit and polish, tiredness; the blessedness of letters and parcels from home and always the anxious, erratic correspondence with the unpredictable Theo.

We were soon classified into trades and a group of us learned we were to take a course on something called RDF. SECRET! – we must not tell outsiders – my correspondents thought I was shooting a terrible line but for once I was not exaggerating. We had to keep mum.

Because there was a backlog of trainees waiting to start the 6-week technical course some of us, after basic training ("square bashing") was finished were posted directly to stations to learn on the job. A chain of mobile stations was being built around the British Isles – this would be extended and modified as the science of Radio Direction Finding grew, and would be re-christened Radar.

I should explain that the Home Chain, as it was called, consisted of small Radar posts which by 1942 lined the entire coastline of the British Isles. It was divided into CHL (Chain Home Low) and CH (Chain Home High) stations, referring to the heights at which their radar beams were set to function. All my postings were to CHL stations, so we were sweeping not only for low-flying aircraft but for shipping including our own convoys and submarines.

Once we picked up a "blip" we passed on its range, bearing and estimated numbers to the Plotting Room inland. These Plotting Rooms, where pretty WAAF push long paddles across huge central tables, supervised by rows of stern, handsome RAF officers seated above them, are always the scenes featured in movies about the war. Not our humble, cramped, cold little cliff-top cabins – oh the injustice! But without our vital input, their work would not have existed.

IT'S ODD, THE THINGS ONE REMEMBERS

Top left: Home Chain Radar station along the northeast coast; I was posted to a succession of these during my 3 years in the WAAF. Below, the radar tubes at which I spent my hours scanning for incoming enemy.

To one of these stations, via another long train journey over unfamiliar ground, I was sent, and found myself at a tiny spot named Trelanvean on the tip of the Cornish peninsula, almost at Land's End. En route we were bedded down in a large house serving as Wing HQ. Our rations for the 2 days' journey lay beside our sleeping bags on the floor and were nibbled on during the night by rats; the first time I had ever met the creatures, but not the last, in the course of Service life.

Trelanvean was lovely. More new friends – interesting and exciting to begin to learn the ropes and to have it slowly dawn on us what in fact we were supposed to be doing. There was time between watches to walk to a neighbouring village and enjoy huge Cornish cream teas, to ride horses on a farm – a brief idyll, because after only five weeks and having seen some of the new friends posted away, my turn came and it was back to the "real" RAF life.

Yatesbury in Wiltshire was a permanent camp, overflowing even its sprawling facilities with the influx of trainees for the new programs. Diary again: "After yet another long cold journey a miserable sixteen of us arrived at this vast place, a second Bridgenorth only far worse. More strict, more lonely, longer hours, no free time – I hate it, and I've never really hated anything before. Six weeks – and one day has seemed an eternity!".

In particular I found the course at the radar school quite mystifying. On the station carrying out allotted tasks in a team had been fairly simple. Learn how to read range and bearings off the screen, plot them on a map, pass them on by telephone, keep a log – what could be more straightforward? But, given a text book full of technical diagrams and terms, a hot lecture hall, an instructor talking of matters quite foreign to me – bewilderment! What are X and Y plates, cathode ray tubes, wavelengths, dipoles? Antennae – surely they belong on the heads of insects?

Eventually enough must have sunk in to enable me to pass, sew the coveted sparks badge on my sleeve, and brace myself for posting time again. Always one hoped to be sent near home, inevitably one was sent farther away. For administration purposes the radar stations came under Fighter Command, which was divided into four Wings covering England, Scotland, Wales and the Isle of Man. The most coveted postings were to 75 Wing in the southeast where all the action was, both on and off duty. For me of course it would also have meant being closer to home. I was destined to spend the next three years on stations in 73 Wing up and down the north-east and east coasts of England. This, though far from home, had its advantages. I could sometimes visit my Yorkshire relatives, and even better, when Theo, now in the Army, was accepted for officers' training he spent several months at the huge base at Catterick, also in north Yorkshire. We could rendezvous by bus or train for occasional getaways – to Durham, to lovely Richmond in the Vale of York, even one magical New Year to Edinburgh. They were typical wartime escapes; emotionally charged, sometimes difficult and frustrating, sometimes simply happy cameos of time.

My first two permanent stations were so small – mobile units perched precariously on windy cliff tops above the grey North Sea – that the personnel were billeted in private homes in adjacent communities. My first eight months were spent at RAF Cresswell, and I lived in the mining village of Lynemouth some miles north of Newcastle. It had been built in the 1930s as a model village. The houses were of yellow brick, identical in size and joined in rows, but laid out in roads and crescents of careful design, centred round shops, community centre, cinema, church, clinic, etc.

Mrs. Murray my landlady was, like her neighbours, bewildered and apprehensive of this invasion of young service people – who was to know if they would be bad or good? Her own two daughters were away in the WAAF and her Army husband was a prisoner of war in Germany. This tiny woman was managing her household of two grown sons, (both working down t'pit and earning good money) and a pale 3-year-old named Anne, child of No. 1 WAAF daughter who had deposited her on mother and returned to her husband-less service life. Mrs. M. gave me her best front bedroom, fed me eggs and sausage and black pudding and strong tea; overcame her misgivings and, I heard later, informed her friends that she had "done all right – 'they' had given her a nice 'un".

My social conscience developed apace in these surroundings. The miners like the farmers were being better paid and taken notice of by a needy government at war, but a great burden lay on the women and older men still working in the pits. The lads, Reg and Eric, they were kings! – money in their pockets, girls galore and no father to keep them in check. Reg and Eric were reasonable enough, and as for little Anne, she became my charge. When not on watch or sleeping I would spend much time with her. I took her to the clinic to collect her free allocation of orange juice and cod liver oil (and more importantly, persuaded Mrs. M. of the need that the child take them). I washed and dressed her and brushed her hair; I helped iron the endless supply of white shirts which the boys demanded be always ready for their evenings off – I helped all I could. Comparing notes with the other billettees I think we all did quite well. Social life was low key – we cycled a lot, including to and from the site; bussed into Newcastle for the "pictures" – as I said, I must have seen more movies in the war years than ever before or since.

Christmas 1942, my first in the service, passed convivially enough; the parade of names in my diary is formidable. Most of them I can remember, and a varied group they were. Postings were so frequent, promises to write, keep in touch and to meet again were always made but hard to maintain after a while. Occasionally there was the pleasure of meeting up again at another station.

Then came another move. Not far, and not very different, this time to live in the dockland area of South Shields on Tyneside, one of Britain's biggest shipbuilding centres. I was billetted with a docker and his wife and daughter, Cynthia, who was my age. Gone was the comfort of Mrs. Murray's best walnut-finish suite and big double bed; I shared Cynthia's tiny room with a foot of space between our two beds. But we got on well enough and our different life styles rubbed off on each other. I was able to convince Cynthia that it is more comfortable to undress completely and get into night clothes at bedtime, rather than put them on over 3 layers of existing underwear. And to persuade Mrs. Payne, though with great difficulty, to go and have her teeth examined. She was in constant pain from decayed teeth but terrified of a dentist. It was not the cost – her husband's insurance was enough – just terror. So I accompanied her once or twice, and by the time I left her treatment was well under way.

By August 1943, just a year after I joined up, my days in private billets were over and I moved into camp. Nissen huts – eating, sleeping, washing and working in a series of them laid out on bare acres of windswept ground. Freezing cold in winter, dust bowls in summer; short on warm bathwater and long on fatigue and still-not-quite conquered homesickness, but bearable throughout due to the camaraderie that "real" service life created. The first such station was RAF Cleadon, near Sunderland – still on that barren north-east coast. While there I passed the much-dreaded Trade Test which elevated me to the rank of Leading Aircraftwoman, able to sew a "props" (propellor) badge on my sleeve above the "sparks".

That however was as far as my promotions went. I was still only 19 and the minimum age for commissioned officers was 20. In any case I was not greatly interested. The officers I knew seemed to be in a constant state of self-repression, caused I suppose by the strictness of their training and their uncertain status beside their male colleagues. Womens' Lib. had not yet totally freed ambitious girls from social restraints, even though in the factories and in the services they were theoretically equal with the men. So, it was as humble 2033382 Bentley, LACW, that I was demobbed two and a half years later, to the disappointment of my ever-ambitious mother who tried hard to persuade me to try for a commission and a possible overseas posting. But by that time my future was turning in a very different direction. I am ahead of my story.

For the past 18 months we on our outposts had been, as it were, coming closer to the war. Tyneside had taken some heavy raids, and our experience expanded rapidly when we found ourselves confusing fishing fleets with incoming low-flying aircraft! We half envied the south coast stations who were so close to the drama of the D Day invasions, the return of troops from Sicily and – less enviable – the introduction by the enemy of the pernicious V1s and V2s – automated little nasties which zoomed in silently and exploded, not silently, without warning because they were too fast to track. At this time my home county of Kent became known as Hell's Corner as it was bearing the brunt of these attacks, and I had the new, unpleasant sensation of being more anxious about my family than they needed to be about me.

Although the operations teams on radar sites were largely female (our RAF counterparts being occupied overseas on mobile sites in North Africa, Cyprus, Sicily and India among other faraway places), our technical staff were increasingly being augmented by Canadians. Canada, in addition to providing huge training programs for RAF pilots, had also created radio training schools, partly for a defence system of its own east and west coasts but also to send needed personnel to Britain. Very good they were. Never could I have dreamt that later I would get to know many RCAF "vets" in their own country; that some would be colleagues of my husband's in Canadian defence programs, and that SIXTY years on we would still be gathering for Radar Reunions in Canada and the U.K.

My final eighteen months in the WAAF (August 1944 – December 1945) were spent at RAF Winterton, near Yarmouth on the coast of East Anglia. Slightly softer in climate and landscape than the dear, dour Northumbrian cliffs, and made pleasant from the start by the rare and happy reunion with three of my closest friends from Cleadon – Pauline, Jeannie, and Daphne. Together we made a quartet of support and affection which has endured all our lifetimes. We met in 1991 at the first Radar Reunion in Coventry. The quality of that meeting, the tears and laughter and endless reminiscences, could only be understood by those who had like us spent our girl-to-woman years in that intense, encapsulated wartime service life.

To Winterton my parents and Bill came for a short summer visit, staying in the village and enjoying the almost-forgotten pleasure of a "seaside" holiday. Most of the British coast was off limits to civilians, so barricaded with barbed wire and gun emplacements as to be an undesirable playground in any case, but we had the freedom of a small stretch of sandy beach and dunes. The cathedral city of Norwich was not far away and made a popular escape. I used to enjoy staying at the very comfortable YWCA hostel which fronted on the cathedral close, attending wonderful services there, wandering the narrow streets and browsing the bookstores, alone or with one of the others. It was a gentler world than the bare-bones industrial towns of Tyneside whose inhabitants had taught me so much and who remain still so vivid to me in memory.

Theo came once or twice to Norwich, as he had done to Lynemouth and Newcastle, but the complexity of our relationship, the lack of clear vision of just what kind of a future we could expect with each other, drove us over some rough emotional country. Briefly one shining weekend we went on leave to Sutton Valence with a ring in his pocket and won, after their previous reluctance, my parents' agreement to our engagement. A few hours of excited planning and a celebration lunch – in the middle of which came a telephone call from Theo's father. Reginald Hancock, a distinguished, talented, wise and sensitive man whom I admired and had grown to love and who Theo would never cross, emphasised, but as gently as he could, that this engagement would be disastrous; we could not and must not take such a step at this time. (Theo was just short of 21, I was 20).

White-faced the poor boy returned to the dinner table and, asking to speak to me alone, led me to my room and gently removed that beautiful little sapphire and diamond band from my finger, repeating as best he could his father's words.

Tears – anguish – dismay – and, most cruel yet understandable, my parents' immediate and total rejection of Theo as the villain of the piece; breaking our child's heart, etc. (To do them justice they later came to agree with the decision; they may even have been relieved. It was the timing and shock which they condemned.)

There was no point in prolonging the leave; I was in any case due to catch a train that afternoon. Theo, ignored and forlorn, slipped away before me; barely a chance for a word of farewell. And, what word could there be? My poor father, always at something of a loss when dealing with emotional storms, had to take me to the station and use the minutes before the train's departure to urge me to hold fast – not subject either of us to any more rollercoasters – "DO NOT GO BACK!"

The weeks that followed were the saddest of my young life. I felt changed, at sea, unable to let go of that sweet companionship, to salvage something, to continue somehow – but how? Even though I knew that Reggie was totally right in that marriage would be a disaster for us. Indeed I had said myself that I didn't expect Theo and I would ever marry, yet as our attachment grew deeper some pledge seemed needed. Hence the attempt at engagement.

We wrote of course – painfully trying to make a slow climb back to a tentative resumption – of what? Of love, since it never really died and became tucked away in a nervous recess of our lives; preserved, unfulfilled, but also undamaged. Theo's parents both wrote to me so that I need not doubt their affection. He had two gold signet rings made, with each others' initials on the insides and outsides. When my mother saw mine she sat heavily down at the kitchen table, shook her head and said – you are incorrigible, Ann! For the fifty-five years of my marriage the ring stayed in its box but now is worn again.

We next met at Victoria station about three months later, when Theo was going on embarkation leave prior to posting to Italy. Dear Edward Atienza was there for moral support – equally for us both! There was a great bouquet of yellow roses; the most ardent and uninhibited kiss

IT'S ODD, THE THINGS ONE REMEMBERS

I had yet received – and our ways parted. Not for ever. We met at intervals both in England and in the USA, where Theo emigrated not long before I too sailed for life in the New World in 1953. And of course we wrote – the form of communication at which we had always been best and free-est.

There is no doubt that many peoples' reservations about our friendship arose from the fact that he had some characteristics which would now label him as gay.

In the black and white schoolboy world, anyone who was artistic, who liked poetry, dancing, acting – was interested in clothes and style – risked being labelled pouf, fairy, queen, or at the most charitable simply a sissy. To a very small degree Theo fit this picture, but he would not have been a school prefect or a respected senior scholar if his personality had been seriously at variance with the perceived "norm." Myself I was not in the least concerned; after all these interests were the very ones we shared, and I had not grown up in a boys' school without knowing how common, sometimes painful, sometimes dangerous, their love affairs could be. In Theo's case I came to understand that he was a person who too often wanted "love" to follow "friendship"; he almost demanded as much commitment from someone who engaged his affection as he bestowed on them. At least two of our mutual male friends said to me in effect: "I simply can't give Theo all the emotional attention he wants. Fond though I am of him I sometimes feel I have to 'get out from under'".

As our own relationship developed there was certainly no doubt at all of his appreciation of my being female; he was a most satisfactory suitor. Just occasionally I sensed a sudden mood swing; could almost feel a closing down, a withdrawal, after a particularly close or happy time. This conflict, and the unhappiness and uncertainty it sometimes engendered, was I am sure well understood by his wise father, and was part of the reason behind Reggie's loving but firm insistence that we postpone any idea of marriage. How Theo's life was affected in later years I could only guess from sporadic correspondence and a handful of meetings.

A complex, gifted, turbulent soul. To know him so well when I was so young gave me a grounding in the psychology of human nature that I might otherwise not have gained until much later in life!

He did marry, but only briefly and with a sudden, unkind ending that left him devastated. He settled in the upper Hudson River valley, home to many artists more famous than he, and pressed me to visit him there. I could and should have done, but by then had allowed my family life to tightly enfold me. When I heard in the early 1990s that he had died quite suddenly I was wracked with guilt, sorrow and self-despising for not having, quite simply, gone. Got in the car and driven through the Eastern Townships and down a stretch of the Adirondacks – a beautiful drive it would have been. But I never did. I was also frustrated beyond measure by my inability to contact anyone who could tell me more about him. I knew no-one from his American life and had no way of finding his sister Elaine, whom I knew to be married and in England and with whom I had been friends in our teens.

Eventually I heard from the kind postmistress in his village, to whom I had written after she returned my last letter marked with the chill notation "deceased" , but all she could tell me was that he had died quite suddenly "some time ago" and that his ashes had been strewn in the Hudson River near where he lived. With that I had to be content but of course it was impossible to be so. Many pages of my diary at that time – February, 1992 – tried to deal with such a raw and deep wound, but the thread which Theo wove through my life is best summed up in this extract:

> "There quite simply has never been anyone else like Theo or in Theo's place in my life. Other friends, other loves, have all been – aside, apart, different. Nothing, either, to do with or interfere with my marriage, he never did. No my dear, you interfered with nothing, you were just there, always . .... Now you have left me,

IT'S ODD, THE THINGS ONE REMEMBERS

and that's all I know, and I weep as much for this dreadful not-knowing as for my bereavement."

But in time of war personal crises, however self-absorbing, could only pale beside the greater dramas which by 1944 were unfolding almost monthly. Indeed, I was thankful to have something to do; to be a tiny thread in that network which, as we learned with pride once the shroud of secrecy was lifted in later years, really had been a major factor in Britain's defence.

In late 1943 came the fall and execution of Benito Mussolini and the Allied invasion of Italy. The Russians were gradually strengthening their hard-won advances across Eastern Europe. The arrival of American forces in Britain raised morale in more ways than the purely military. Army units appeared in Norfolk and cheerful GIs came to our dances and invited us to theirs. I did not befriend any particularly, but those I met were generous with gifts, informal and breezily interested in this quaint old country. They seemed to us like louder and larger versions of our now-familiar Canadians.

Then of course the justification for this mighty American presence was revealed in the tense days of early June 1944 when Operation Overlord was launched, France invaded through the beaches of Normandy and the final Allied advance across Western Europe begun. By August Paris was liberated and General Charles de Gaulle led his Free French troops, so long exiled in Britain, through the Arc de Triomphe – avec quelle grande triomphe. Hopeful days for a tired world, ally and enemy alike so weary of tragedy and loss.

Our own family's first casualty that summer was none other than the father of my little godson Tom – my cousin Renee's beloved Dawson, killed in Normandy by a bomb on the post he was commanding. Within two days I received two telegrams from home. The first was to say that Renee had just borne a new son. It was followed within 12 hours by the second, telling me of Dawson's death. The new David had in fact been born two days after his father was killed, but the news had been kept from Renee to give her a space of joy with the babe.

Over the previous three years we had of course mourned a number of fallen Old Boys from school as well as other friends; we worried over those who were prisoners of war, especially in the Far East; over cousin David, the new David's uncle, who was with the Durham Light Infantry in India; over Theo, from whom small Italian gifts and notes still trickled in. But Dawson Whaley, a most quiet and gentle man in contrast to the mercurial and passionate Renee, was a cruel personal loss to us all. At the height of my "golden year " of 1942-43 when she and Tommy and his sister Mary were living with my family, and she and mama were closely observing the progress of my rocky romance, Renee said to me "you'll see; you and I will both be widows before this war is over". I don't know if she believed it or whether she was trying obliquely to deflate any ideas of marriage I might have had. Certainly I never believed even she would be widowed.

But she was. She did marry again, a neighbour and old friend of both her and Dawson's families, who brought her a loving stepdaughter and much contentment until he too died. Renee lives alone in a grey stone house in the grey stone town of Hawes at the head of Wensleydale, at 87 reclusive but almost as outspoken as ever. A few years ago Tom was able to visit his father's grave in France, which gave him and his mother a measure of satisfaction and peace.

Thus the end of 1944 found me wrung out emotionally, physically and psychologically. I think I had grown up somewhat. I had developed a "social conscience" (which in fact had been embryonic since about the age of 14), nurtured now by my months spent among the miners and dockers of the North East. It was to help make my life more interesting and lead me on paths that I had not been expected by my family to travel. It is interesting to note that in my final diary entry of that year I wrote:

"I have had more than enough of so profitless a life. I find myself at moments in a kind of panic at the time I am wasting here. A longing to

IT'S ODD, THE THINGS ONE REMEMBERS

get on, on with the things I have at length decided I can and want to do. Are we all perhaps straining for a glimpse of the end of a war that has dragged on so long?"

Maybe, but there were still months of struggle ahead. Attention was turning, in those last months to the Pacific naval battles, the bitter ground operations in Burma and Indonesia, bringing wider and sinister recognition of that most evil enemy still to be dealt with – Japan. Certainly the European fronts were pincering in from the west and from the east, albeit slowly, but the Germans were still well dug in on the coasts of the Netherlands, peppering south and east England with the aforementioned V1 and V2 rockets – one more unwelcome weight on shoulders already bowed by more than three years of attacks from the skies. I wrote frequently of being very, very tired; my chief memories of the long, devious, dirty train journeys home on leave are that I was almost too bone weary to look forward to it. Once there of course I mostly recovered. As well as the joy of being welcomed there was always the physical bliss of cleanliness, space, colour – "my own pretty room, the house so polished and full of flowers; no uniform for six whole days – and FOOD!"

I do not to this day know how my mother stretched the available supplies to feed not only a ravenous WAAF but a succession of visitors – the transient crowds of wartime bodies always on their way to somewhere else. I shudder to recollect the thoughtless abandon with which I "invited" friends or issued glib orders to fellow service people to "drop in on my parents if you are in that part of the world" And so they did, and were always welcome. She managed, I suppose, as she approached all aspects of her working life, by planning ahead, careful organisation, and disciplined work. I was always so proud to share my beloved home and village; for them to be a haven for others as they were for me.

Early in 1945 RAF Winterton was expanded to house a new, even more hush-hush branch of radar detection. We knew only that it was named Oboe and that a number of ex-overseas technical staff and operators had come to work on it. Some time in April my three inseparables and I went to a station dance to look over some of these new faces. We were sitting, surveying the floor with interest, when suddenly one of them appeared smiling in front of me and asked me to dance. So flustered was I – still and only a humble LACW – by the broad ring of a Flying Officer on his sleeve and the ribbon of the Africa Star on his chest, that I could only move automatically out onto the floor with him, registering little more than the striking dark blue eyes and finely marked brows, plus the fact that he was a beautiful dancer, far better than I. Some months later I was to see those brows and eyes on his mother's face, and years on again carbon copied on that of his daughter.

The dance was short, the evening ended – I am sure there must have been our usual post-mortem in the bungalows afterwards but all I remember is someone remarking – I see Smitty nabbed you, Bentley!

The next day while on watch I received a telephone call apologising for having asked me to dance "before being properly introduced"! Given the informal atmosphere of service life this was a quaint gesture, and I was impressed as well as surprised. Apparently he had asked his mess-mate to introduce him to me but Wattie, who had known me since my flighty Cleadon days and who considered himself something of a pater-familias to us four, had refused. "She has had too many ups and downs recently – I don't want her hurt any more" was apparently the gist of his refusal. (Why, I wondered, would he think that I might be hurt by this apparently straightforward person?). So, characteristically, the blue eyed F.O. had taken matters into his own hands.

This then was Vernon Smith. A 24-year-old technical officer just returned from 5+ years in the North African desert where he had been "chasing Rommel back and forth with our mobile units". Nineteen when he left his home town on the edge of the Black Country, his education barely completed, he found in the developing world of radar the ideal climate for his deep interest in all aspects of scientific technology. His abilities were recognised and earned him an early commission.

(The R.A.F., youngest and most democratic of all the British services, looked first at a person's worth rather than his social background, his family or his old school tie.) By the age of 23 he was Commanding Officer of a station on Cyprus; a pleasant change from the sand and tents of the desert. Thence, a few months previous to our meeting, he had been returned to England.

Smitty

What did we like about each other? In every way he was the opposite of the late lamented Theo. Practical, uncompromising, with the almost ruthless honesty of his blunt Lancashire forbears, he already knew where he was going and what he wanted. I must have seemed a fey kind of creature, with my poetry and my chattiness and my complicated emotional life, but he sought my company and we began to spend off-duty times together – circumspectly, because even the tolerance of the Air Force didn't extend to condoning inter-rank socialisation. Bicycle rides mostly, or bus rides into Yarmouth for the inevitable cinema and fish and chip suppers. Walks on the reedy dunes north of the Officers' Mess, which was a private house away from the station, near the hamlet of Winterton. This consisted of a large church, some small houses, and of course a pub, The Three Mariners, which was to take its place in our history four months later.

To me his uncomplicated, friendly company was immensely soothing. I felt becalmed after the storms and sorrows of the previous year. Writing a few months later to an old school friend I said I had met the kind of man "whose slippers I would be happy to have waiting by the fire". To which Janet wryly and very astutely replied "Isn't it a bit early in life to be thinking about fireside slippers?"

Whatever. The fact was that by April 1945 events so momentous were crowding in that everyone, old friends as well as new, were caught up in them. On 13th April Franklin Roosevelt died. It was sadly ironic that he, responsible eventually for the entry of the United States into the war, should not live that extra month to see it ended in Europe. Services were held throughout Britain, including in our parish church at Winterton. I remember that Vernon and I went off on our bikes afterwards (free day) and lay in a hayfield chewing the long sweet grasses and pondering the speed at which changes were coming. On 27th April the American and Russian armies joined forces at the River Elbe; on the 30th, with the Russians fighting street by street through Berlin, Hitler committed suicide. "What a day to wake upon, when that man is dead and gone!". During the first week of May there were surrender documents signed in Italy, on Luneberg Heath, in Reims, and the War in Europe officially ended on 8th May.

Celebrations on the station spread over several days – the fact that Vernon's birthday was on the 9th just added to the cheer. But in the previous week we had been to London for a more personal celebration – my 21st birthday party. I had asked for, and my generous parents had provided, a dinner/dance/theatre evening, hoping for a gathering of many friends, but of course only a few were available, and those more of my parents' generation than my own. We were finally ten in number. Anne Fletcher was far away but her parents came to represent

IT'S ODD, THE THINGS ONE REMEMBERS

her, and Robin Burns stood in for the S.V.S. gang. Three other lifelong friends; mother and father – in all eight loving supporters to be introduced to the new RAF acquaintance.

The dinner was at the Savoy Hotel and I was thrilled to have Carol Gibbons and his dance band playing for me – well known at the time but now part of ballroom dance history. Then on to the play, "The Lady From Edinburgh" at the Playhouse Theatre, then on, very late, to a small hotel in Knightsbridge where my father had been able to find three minute rooms, one for themselves, one for Robin and Vernon and one for Mary P. and me. (Mary P., whose house was ONE MILE from my home and whom I had known since infancy. She became godmother to my daughter and is still a loyal friend.) We walked there under the stars, laughing and singing for the magic which permeated London in that amazing week – as if it were holding its breath.

Back next day to work and the realisation that it all really was coming to an end, though at such cost and with such vast problems ahead. "Peace coming not with a clarion call but in pieces". Who said that? I don't remember, but if there is an end there must then be a beginning, and we could not help feeling that now we could look ahead, make a start, even if there were a lot of those pieces to be picked up along the way.

Now began the process of closing down or amalgamating the stations of the radar chain. Only two sections remained open at Winterton, the Admin. one – we still had to be paid, fed and housed – and the technical supplies. The immediate question regarding operators was, how to keep us occupied? Some brain coined a word which I have ever since considered the ultimate euphemism – MIS-EMPLOYMENT. So, mis-employed we became in a variety of ways, along with grumbling, mirth, resignation, and a consuming interest in the start of the de-mobbing process – demobilisation. Priorities were logical enough – length of service, age, married or single. Those put me near the bottom of the pile, but there were compensations. Much more free time, glorious sunny weather, the novelty of odd occupations. I had a short, exhausting, but interesting stint in the cookhouse, learning to measure flour in 50 lb. bags, potatoes in hundredweight sacks, milk in gallons. I once deep-fried a huge batch of doughnuts which to my chagrin my friends condemned outright – "you burned them!".

Vernon and I cycled ever farther afield, refreshed by powerful Norfolk cider in the pubs, and learned to sail in elementary fashion in the heavy old boats that were for hire on the Broads. We went to Norwich on a weekend pass which I overstayed, thereby getting myself put on a charge. I can't remember what form the punishment took but that my WAAF commanding officer finished her lecture by saying – "you know Bentley, with a good record like yours, it just wasn't worth it". I did not dare tell her that it had been so. I was ashamed and embarrassed thus to have blotted my copybook, but Vernon just laughed. To him the system – any system – was there to be challenged; obeyed only so far as necessary. In the same spirit he talked me out of going ahead with an application for a commission. "You don't want to be stuck in this outfit any longer than you have to. I can think of better things for you to do."

IT'S ODD, THE THINGS ONE REMEMBERS

So much for my conscientious adherence to the status quo, and for mother's ambitions for me. We went to Sutton Valence on leave, he was welcomed as were all my friends, but he observed later that "I don't think your mother liked me all that much." I pointed out that mother probably felt somewhat cautious when presented with a new male in my life. One might think that with Theo disposed of she would welcome newcomers but, still holding very definite ideas about the kind of person I should marry, she wasn't prepared to greet Vernon with open arms.

Then in early August came the dropping of the atomic bombs on Hiroshima and Nagasaki, the surrender of the Japanese to the Americans and the true end of the war. This of course removed the dread we had all summer of our remaining forces being sent to the Far East – Vernon among them. So, after much hesitation and uncertainty on my part (but none whatever on his – his mind was made up) – we became officially engaged and had a large, cheerful celebration at the Three Mariners, a heady combination of the euphoria of the war's end and our personal happiness.

By some process of self-immersed thoughtlessness I did not tell my parents of my engagement or of this party until afterwards. I could not – I still cannot – begin to find an explanation. I am sure this was not characteristic of me – had not my whole life been shared and bound up with them? I can only think such selfishness was the product of the divide between service and home life that had grown over the previous three years. I was living, absorbed, in the former while the latter was for the present set aside. So – my beloved mother and father, who had already spent much effort and expense on my wonderful birthday party, were not only left out of the celebration of my engagement but unaware of it until it was over. Their shock and hurt threw a deserved shadow over my happiness; in fact for some weeks to come I was less than happy at all. "And you expect us to rejoice over an engagement of which we were not only ignorant but to which, had we been consulted, we would have strenuously objected; which in fact had you been under 21 we would have forbidden?"

In general terms, they simply thought I was not ready for marriage. Still so passionately and closely tied to them and their home; still, in spite of much evidence to the contrary, they thought me emotionally bound to Theo. In more particular and emphatic terms, Vernon was not the person they wanted me to marry. Interestingly, one of mother's voiced objections was "I don't think you can make him happy. The kind of person who, were it not for the war, you would never have met." (Yet into that very war she had urged me, hoping to extend my range of acquaintances....!) All this quite apart from the unvoiced objections which I well knew already: the wrong background/education/family/upbringing.

To their enormous credit they remained steadfastly loyal to me, and in time to us both, through the many challenges we were to face. They learned to recognise Vernon's steadfastness, to admire his fine brain and his success in his career, to value him as the dedicated family man, the "good provider" that he certainly was, to love our children and eventually make several happy visits to us in Canada.

Meanwhile they gave me as fine a wedding day as I could wish for. Any restrictions to its splendour were due to wartime difficulties of supply rather than restraint or reluctance on their part.

We were married at Sutton Valence on 13th October, 1945 – the date, my lucky 13th, defiantly chosen by me. The parish church of St. Mary's is solid and unbeautiful but stands high on the western ridge of the village, overlooking the Weald. About two hundred family, friends and villagers lined the path to the lychgate to cheer us – a path which Daddy, rising early that morning, had cleared of straying rose brambles that might have caught in my veil. The school choir sang, our old friend the school chaplain married us and the reception was held in School Hall. My connections to my roots were all in place, even at this first symbolic severance of them.

Despite our differences mama and I had had pleasure, even excitement in the preparations, every stage of which challenged one's ingenuity in such times of shortage. Enough coupons for a plain white crepe wedding dress, yes. But not for a veil; I borrowed one of Anne's; nor for an outfit for mother of the bride – she borrowed a smart pale blue suit from a friend. Knowing I would not be able to dress a team of bridesmaids, I opted for a single one and chose Vernon's 12-year-old second cousin Sheila thereby avoiding strife among my own army of Banks/Bentley relatives. For Sheila also we borrowed a dress; with a silver net Juliet cap, slippers and a Victorian posy she looked and acted perfectly. Her father, Vernon's cousin Sandford, was best man. Bill, now just 13, wore as mentioned earlier his first pair of long trousers, his school jacket and straw boater. Daddy in tails, of course, and his legendary top hat. (Legendary because it had a long life and was sometimes produced on occasions not wholly appropriate; it had last graced his bald head at a Maidstone school prize giving when I, aged eight, won a form prize for the first and last time in my life. Fortunately I was young enough to be proud, not embarrassed, by this eccentricity).

Then, how to get enough ingredients for even a small wedding cake? By pooling rations, gratefully accepting offers from friends, eggs from a poultry-raising aunt, and extras otherwise quite unobtainable from the school catering department… Even professional photographers were restricted by the amount of film and paper available, and could only offer an album of limited size and number of prints. But they were good photographs. (Twenty years later in suburban Ottawa a group of neighbours had the idea of a wedding album coffee party. How overshadowed was my faded, cardboard-covered wartime album by those dazzling satin and silver creations, fat with many coloured pictures! But how greatly interested and impressed were their owners by my almost historic offering.)

Even the ring presented difficulties. Jewellers had to work on "allocations" – Vernon and I went into Maidstone and brought home a plain 9kt. gold job at which Mother Smith threw up her hands and said, "That's no good! take it back; I'll get you a real ring." And so she did, as she acquired many things from mysterious sources about which one asked no questions. An unusual narrow, graceful octagon engraved with a design which, like the eight corners, has long since worn away – but which is made of 24kt. gold, no less. Where did she get it? I'll never know, but I've never seen one like it.

Vernon wore uniform and looked fine; I most certainly did not (wear uniform) and defied convention by choosing a black wool suit for my "going-away" costume – terribly bad luck to wear black to a wedding my dear. But it was smart and I loved it, and completed it with a pillbox hat of pink feathers and a blouse also pink with big tie bow. On the train from London to Devon next day I spilled tomato soup on the bow - but it was nearly the same colour, Vernon said.

We had been almost reluctant to leave the party which followed the reception, because so many family and friends, some of whom we had not seen for years or had never met, had made the effort to come. But we had rooms booked at a hotel in Woolacombe – again, thanks to a friend of a friend – and seaside accommodations were scarce, almost all occupied still by service people, so off we went, tin cans tied to the back of the car by Bill and friends, clanging away up the Lower Road. Out of sight of the house, our driver and Vernon removed them, and for want of any other receptacle, mailed them in the village letter box. We never heard that there were any repercussions.

A week by the sea passed quickly, then back to misemployment again, softened by happy memories and anticipation of our own demobbing. But still between me and my precious parents the strands of our close bond had been broken and our relationship changed. Letters from mother – and all my life from the age of five there had been letters; so many, so frequent, so long – which might previously have begun "My darling child" now were coolly addressed to "My dear Ann". Following my demobilisation in early December I lived at home waiting until Vernon also should be out of the RAF. This period, so eagerly looked forward to for three years, was instead a painful time. I longed to "explain myself" to M and D –to try to tell them how my conviction of the rightness of my choice must surely outweigh their disappointment. That I intended to make a success of my life with Vernon and prove it to them.

IT'S ODD, THE THINGS ONE REMEMBERS

But for a long time, over the superficially smooth routines, this newly built wall stood between us and frank discussion was tacitly avoided.

Nevertheless I had begun my own new and important married life and that needed my interest and energy. I had of course met Vernon's parents, Jim and Lilian; his lively cousins and the formidable Uncle Albert, family patriarch. He the driving force who, with his gentler brother Jim had the courage to leave the poverty of their native Lancashire and establish a small but prospering cotton mill in Dudley. They were all welcoming and helpful to me; Lilian and Jim, like my own parents, supported and helped us in all our adventures and endeavours to come.

Vernon was less fortunate than I in his demobbing, having to wait until the spring of 1946. He hated every minute of the remaining months; longing only to be "shot of" the RAF, he was instead given the arduous job of closing down what was left of the Winterton site. Himself the only officer, he had a sergeant and one or two bods to help him with the tedious, complex task of making an inventory of every last piece of equipment from blankets ("if the numbers didn't tally we tore the blankets in half to make more") to firearms. He was short a pair of pistols, and this caused so much fuss, paperwork, calls from Wing HQ and visits from equally harried superiors that he became physically ill and developed acute stress-related abdominal pains. Only frequent weekend leaves helped somewhat. Eventually the pistols were accounted for – whether in their rightful place or not he didn't by then care – he obtained his discharge and Service life was behind us at last.

Never really to be forgotten, of course. It had shaped us and our friends, it had educated us, brought us together, created bonds many of which would last our lifetimes. In our minds and our memories those years were always somehow in our sight – and of course have now been so documented, in history and in endless personal recollections, as to define our generation. But we were still a young generation. For all of us the priority now was work; for those who had not begun their careers before the war, how to embark on one, and equally pressing, how to find a place to live.

NINA ANN SMITH

Vernon's parents, Jim Smith and Lillian (nee Drake), were unfailingly generous to us in our poorer, early years of marriage.

Our wedding, Sutton Valence, 1945; my father in his famous top hat; this time worn appropriately.

CHAPTER 4

WORCESTERSHIRE AND LONDON

Vernon's family with a practical generosity typical of them had created a small flat for us in the annex to their factory in Dudley. This was a big redbrick Victorian house named Russell's Hall and it stood on a rise outside the town, a lovely neglected garden and crumbing wall around it, and a view westward towards the Clent hills, across the fields where Vernon used to play as a child. The flat was perfect. A big living room with a floor-to-ceiling window, small bedroom, kitchen, bathroom, all skilfully adapted from an unused upstairs floor and renovated and painted just for us. Few newly-weds at that time could have been so lucky. As to furnishing it – parents to the rescue again, lending tables and chairs and advising on the best way to invest precious coupons and "units" on such utility furniture as was available.

So one September Sunday in Sutton Valence we loaded a small van with our wedding presents, my father's old tin trunk and Vernon's battered RAF one from his Middle East travels, tied the doors precariously shut with rope, and drove away. Up the Lower Road from Bentley's House, past the letter box where 11 months before we had stowed the tin cans from our wedding car – up and away from Sutton Valence.

Uncle Albert gave Vernon a job as floor supervisor at the factory, overseeing a band of tough local women who regarded him tolerantly as but a lad – both he and they saw the humour of it. Equally did the family know quite well that this would be only an interim arrangement and that Vernon's sights were set on a different future. But how and where to find it?

He and I spent the next few months, snugger and warmer in our centrally heated nest than most of Britain in that bitterly cold winter of 1946, contemplating our options. Vernon knew that his best prospects would be to develop the technological knowledge he had begun to acquire in the RAF, but for that he ("only a grammar school boy") would need further training. We contacted various ex-service colleagues, answered advertisements, drew on my father's expertise as Careers Master at Sutton Valence, and came to the conclusion that he would need to take evening classes towards the necessary qualifications to sit the exams for the Professional Institute of Engineers. In early 1947 he was offered a post in the laboratories of Standard Telecommunications in Middlesex and at the same time found that the courses he needed were available at a north London college of the University of London.

So – London! But where would we live? Into storage in a spare room of Lil and Jim's house went most of our few possessions, homes were found for our lovely cats, Stumpy and Mouse, and off we went again with our two tin trunks. No family could have been more tolerant of, or helpful to, a pair "in transition" such as we were. They had given us a comfortable, needed space of time to accustom ourselves to each other, to civilian life, to think through our future plans without distractions, all the while knowing that we were not there to stay. We made our gratitude and appreciation as clear as we could and were to have many further instances of their helpfulness as time went on.

We found lodgings in Surbiton, a very respectable south London suburb – a long way from where Vernon really needed to be, but all accommodation was still scarce. We had two tiny rooms at the top of Mrs. Figgis' house – a gas ring for cooking, three pounds a week and extra for the use of the iron in her kitchen and space in her refrigerator. Despite her name she was very French, and kept a sharp eye on the household accounts. Mr. Figgis was rarely seen except in the garden.

The summer of 1947 was as hot and sunny as the previous winter had been bitter. Vernon cycled to the station for a long journey by tube and bus to Potter's Bar, as far north of the city as Surbiton was south As for me, although I realised how necessary had been the months of adjustment in the Dudley flat, I felt I had been too long unemployed. I found a part time secretarial job and soon I too was cycling to the station every day for a short ride to a Life Insurance Company in Teddington. Dull, but some facts about insurance did rub off on me and came in useful in later life!

We were then, and for the next three or four years, decidedly short of money. I brought to my marriage forty pounds in War Savings Certificates, Vernon had a proportionately larger sum therein, and his wages. His always generous family had charged us no rent for the Russell's Hall flat, as well as paying him more than the strict value of his short stint at the Scrim factory – a small family factory where cotton muslin fabric was manufactured. Now that generosity extended further when they offered to buy us a house, on which we would pay a very reasonable rent until we could either buy it or move elsewhere.

It was time to have a house of our own for many reasons. Not only the obvious desire to "settle down" but to wean me once and for all from this still compelling attachment, this backward-looking-over-my-shoulder, to Sutton Valence and my family there. I was shocked on re-reading the diaries of these years to see that I still referred to it as "home". Despite our shortage of money I made frequent visits there, sometimes with Vernon, more often not, or trips to join mama in London for a play – that and my fare both paid by her, I suppose. I even joined M and D and some friends for a week's holiday in the Lake District, but it fell so far short of the idyllic remembered walking holidays of my schooldays that I wished I had not gone. I rushed down to S.V. for all the school events I could manage – Speech Days, Sports Days, school plays. Bill at 15 was now moving up the school and doing well; Old Boys home from the war were often visiting…..I simply was not giving Vernon or my marriage my full attention. His patience and forbearance in those early years was greater than I deserved. I vowed to myself that I loved him and we were certainly growing closer; we both took a lot of pleasure and satisfaction in home making and both knew how much we needed a place of our own.

Moreover, my negligence must have been less that I feared because the warm summer months in "Figgis Crescent" (Vernon's sobriquet, of course) worked their particular magic and produced the most cogent reason of all for getting a house – the conception of John David.

We had deliberately avoided pregnancy while we lacked "real" jobs or a home, even though some thought two years to be a long time childless. In reply to a letter from me extolling the joys of our two new kittens, Anne had written " I don't want to hear about cats – what about babies?" (she with my second godson already born and his next brother on the way). But in this as in so many other matters we had the benefit of mother's foresight and advanced thinking. I myself had arrived nine months and one day after her wedding in August 1923, and in her autobiography she describes her frustration and disappointment that this "inconvenience" should so have clouded her first year. Not that the baby was received with anything less than total love and devotion, but Nell had hoped for time to adjust to her new life far from her own family, and to help her very young husband do the same in his first teaching post. So she determined that this calamity would not happen to any daughter of hers and she kept abreast of the latest developments

IT'S ODD, THE THINGS ONE REMEMBERS

in birth control, or family planning as it was then less bluntly named, as they came along. Soon after my engagement she made an appointment for me at a London clinic, one of few in the country at that time. As a result I came to my marriage properly equipped and informed. Both Vernon (who always liked to be in control of all aspects of his life if he possibly could) and I were thoroughly satisfied with this arrangement and rather smugly prided ourselves henceforth on the fact that our infants, with one exception, did indeed arrive "as planned".

We moved into 106 Willow Road, Enfield, in September of 1947. It was – may well still be – a semi-detached 3-bedroom villa of a standard type; two front bay windows, straight short path from front gate to door, a side path round to the narrow back garden, shed and back door. The road ran dead straight for over half a mile, from the centre of Enfield almost to the Common, and there were about two hundred houses so we were roughly two-thirds of the way up. No buses ran that way, so all groceries, luggage, baby carriages, guests and commuters walked its length, or if not too burdened we bicycled. The houses were identical except for individual choices of paint and, of course, CURTAINS. These played an important part in suburban furnishings and to the knowing eye told quite a bit about the owner. I remember being torn between my desire to conform and be respectable (two pairs of heavy drapes to close at dark, with sheer net or lace gathered neatly across in the daytime), and my own instincts, which were to make do with skimpy lengths of wartime-saved material, pulled right back to let in all available light.

Mass-produced villa or not, we were enormously happy and relieved to be there, and my parents were as grateful for Lil and Jim's generosity as were Vernon and I. The house was well built and affordable and we were, by post-war standards, very lucky to have it. I think the Smiths paid about 2,000 pounds for it and sold it two and a half years later for a profit of two or three hundred pounds. Father Jim came to stay for a week to re-paint and repair. We had to learn about electricity bills, roof maintenance, plumbing hazards such as freezing pipes, hot water tanks and a mysterious invention called a back boiler. If you kept a fire going in the sitting room grate it heated water in a lead-lined tank behind the chimney. Great – if you had the fuel, the time and the energy to maintain the fire.

There were no other mod. cons. as we came to know them in Canada. No built-in closets or kitchen cupboards, no laundry facilities, central heating, workshop or garage. One upstairs bathroom; in the kitchen no more than an electric cooking stove and a sink. Electricity heated a small water tank (when without the fire for the back boiler) and, though barely, the rooms with an assortment of small heaters of varying efficiency. Sheets, towels, shirts, were sent to a laundry, the rest was done in the kitchen sink and hung out in the garden. One of the most needed presents the new baby received was one of the most modest; a small hand wringer which could be clamped onto the side of the sink to deal with the loads of nappies.

But a house so equipped was the norm for most people. We made good friends with a laboratory colleague of Vernon's and his wife who lived in a similar house a few roads away, and neighbours were friendly enough, though a little wary of the young newcomers. Such friends as had cars were considered prosperous – but lack of a car did not trouble me. I had spent my life travelling by train or bus, bicycle and foot, and I went on doing so. We joked that the treks up and down Willow Road contributed to my healthy, problem-free pregnancy.

Healthy it was – well monitored by the local clinic, well nourished by extra half rations of meat, eggs and milk and the free orange juice and cod liver oil (!) to which expectant mothers were entitled. The next eight months of autumn, winter and spring were serene if hard-working. For Vernon the workload was three-fold. He took evening courses four out of five nights entailing long bus rides after work, and brought home several hours of study at weekends. I was occupied enough by the need to juggle rations and money, little enough of either, to feed and furnish us, but I still wanted to either get a part-time job again or take in a lodger. Eventually both came to pass, but not until after the baby was born and had been with us awhile.

All in all 1947 ended on hopeful notes for us. Our future, which had lacked shape or direction during and since the war was now assuming the very real shape of job, home and family. But for the country it had been a grey year. The war was two years ended, but unrest and confusion were still rife in Europe. I wrote, presumably accurately though with some exaggeration, of "a web of Communism meshing across the continent" and "…and Palestine becoming – what? We know the ageless bitterness of the Arab/Jewish struggle for their contested land. But does it help that struggle to throw bombs into houses or to shoot a man as he stands over his son's grave?"

To 1948. The baby was due on the first of May, which as my father liked unnecessarily to emphasise, is Labour Day to any good socialist. By then Willow Road was transformed into an avenue of arching pink foam, the ornamental cherry trees which lined its pavements were massed in blossom. The cot which had welcomed my brother sixteen years before had been painstakingly trimmed by my mother in yards upon yards of white Scrim – that ubiquitous soft gauze manufactured on the Dudley looms and on which all the Smith households heavily depended, for everything from dishcloths to curtains! Offered the gift of a new pram by Lil and Jim I set my heart on a full size carriage, in spite of their gently pointing out how much more convenient a folding, soft-bodied one would be, given lack of storage space and a bus-dependent lifestyle. But I passionately wanted that big pram; had been eying and comparing them at the clinic and around the shops. So it arrived, big and royal blue with a black leather hood and white wheels. It occupied entirely the narrow front hall and waited there, shiny and splendid, for its occupant.

As did we all. The first of May came and went, so did Vernon's birthday on the 9th and mine on the 13th; the Nursing Home had to change the dates of my booking; friends sent encouraging postcards and Vernon cycled off to the station each day wondering if he would be

called home early. A laburnum tree bloomed, gloriously yellow, in our tiny back garden – the cherry blossoms lingered, waiting too. Vernon had to tackle exams with the other major distraction still to come. And I chanted the anthem of late deliverers the world over –
I feel I have been pregnant for EVER!

On Wednesday May 19th the baby made it known very early on this sunny, still morning that he was on his way, but he was not in the world until about 19 hours later, when it was dark and cool again after the hot day. Knowing well that first labours can be long I was somewhat prepared for it, but even so became weary, as did the nurses, with the effort we were expending with no apparent progress. When he was finally born "with a healthy cry" and was whisked away without my seeing him I was too inexperienced – and probably too tired – to be concerned. In any case that was often the practice in those more clinical, impersonal days before maternity wards became family gathering places.

But next day I did become very concerned, and frustrated and impatient when I still had not seen either my son – "he is resting" – or my husband – "he is talking to Dr. Toop." I could HEAR their voices outside my room. On and on they seemed to go, murmur, murmuring. Why did they not come and include me in whatever they were talking about so long?

At last it was left to Vernon, brave and weary, wondering what on earth had hit him, to come and sit with me and tell me gently but accurately what had befallen us and our baby. He was born with a rare and at that time incurable abnormality in which the hole at the base of the skull, which normally drains cerebral fluid away through the spinal cord, is closed or non-existent. The fluid enlarges the skull, putting pressure on the brain. But he was already probably blind, would not develop any other faculties or probably live beyond his second birthday.

Hydrocephalus – water on the brain.

IT'S ODD, THE THINGS ONE REMEMBERS

Thirty years later a Canadian surgeon perfected an operation, referred to as a shunt, which drained the excess fluid and in some cases enabled the child to develop normally (depending on the degree of damage already done, in utero or at birth). But we had no Canadian surgeon, no shunt. We had John David, who when at last we were allowed to see him didn't look at all bad to us. Certainly there was too heavy a head, too slight a body – maybe that high forehead was inherited from his cerebral father! He had a small, pretty face, blue Smith eyes and an endearing tuft of blond hair sweeping up from his crown. It stayed so all his life.

We took him home, to the support of four loving grandparents as bewildered as we. We roped the fine new pram on the top of a taxi and drove to Victoria Station, thence to Sutton Valence and his christening in the school chapel. To us – to me in particular – he was simply the new expected baby whose needs must be met and his routine followed as any other's would be. This immersion in the everyday and the need to recover my own strength probably kept me balanced, but looking back as a grandparent myself I can see even more clearly what a blow this diagnosis must have been to them. As also to family and friends who, once their automatic congratulations had poured in, had to be told the story – told over and again. To young, proud Uncle Bill... I still have a postcard he sent to John David Vernon-Smith, Esq. It has a sketch of a small infant in a large pram and the words "with his uncle's love". It raises my tears to look at it, to this day.

We took the baby to Dr. Sheldon, a high and mighty gentleman who at that time was one of the obstetricians to the Royal Family and had his office in Harley Street, the highest and mightiest medical address in London. (WHO obtained and paid for that private appointment? Those same who paid for the nursing home, the pram, the taxi, the train fares. Did they wonder when it would ever end? Again with the eyes of a grandparent, I can say no, they did not. They simply carried on, with us and for us.)

Dr. S. competent and concerned, pointed out that the head had not grown much in six weeks; it was possible the damage might be less than first thought; "take him home and make him strong."

He did thrive; he nursed well, slept, gained weight, listened but clearly looked at nothing, just turned his head towards sound. But at the first visit to the doctor who had delivered him (and who had never encountered his like before; no wonder the babe was whisked away so fast) and on a subsequent visit to Dr. Sheldon, both confirmed sadly that indeed his head was expanding and that there was no realistic chance of any progress. "It is time to consider his – and your – futures" the wise men said.

Our future seemed divided into the immediate – to look after Johnnie – and the long term –to carry on with our plans and our family. "Do not despair, your daughter is made for having babies" Dr. Toop had heartily tried to reassure mama. All the more reason for the anguished protest, Why us? Healthy stock, healthy people, chance

IT'S ODD, THE THINGS ONE REMEMBERS

victims of a random blip in the statistics. But we didn't dwell too often on the Why. There was not time. I shelved any idea of job or lodgers, kept busy, got well, took the baby visiting and met with varying reactions. Discomfort, sympathy, honest expressions of grief – revealing insights into the human reaction to the abnormal.

It was at the clinic that the nurse first broached the idea of an institutional placement. Baby was becoming harder to care for; restless, sleeping less, never comfortable. Yet, he was – there – I talked to and played with him, and read to him as unfailingly as I was to read to all my children from their earliest days. On Christmas Day he lay quiet for so long I had to keep checking on him. The unaccustomed peaceful hours were, I have always believed, a gift of God to us for that day.

So, NO was my immediate answer to the nurse's suggestion, but at my next clinic visit she quietly handed me a card with the name of a hospital in Essex "who will be pleased to give you an appointment if you should just want to go and look." It became a matter of an unbalanced scale. Up in the air, on the "light" side was Johnnie, unknowing, unseeing, unhappy, becoming more nearly unalive. Crashing down on the "heavy" side was everything we stood to lose by struggling on with him. Our physical and mental strengths, Vernon's ability to concentrate on the intensive amount of work he needed to do; above all our desire to have another child, which I thought myself unable to handle in addition to this baby. All he needed now was kindly care. It may be that his first weeks of life, loved and cherished in his own home, made him briefly stronger than he would have been without them, but was it a kindness to prolong this effort to give him a "normal" babyhood when he could not be aware of, let alone benefit from it?

Thus we did go to the South Ockendon Hospital, entering for the first time a world with which we were to become very familiar, but which only a small part of the population ever sees; the world inhabited by the "subnormal" among us. In years to come I learned the statistics, the medical facts, the psychology of mental deficiency and its myriad levels and varieties. But on the 21st of April, 1949, all I cared about was how well my child would be tended in that world.

We were driven in a government-supplied car with a government-supplied health worker, presumably for moral support. We handed Johnnie over to a kind sister (they were all so bloody kind) – I fretted that I had not told them what he liked to eat, and that they thought me heartless because I asked for his clothes back. But they had dressed him in a neat blue smock, and after all it was my best layette, and I would need it again, wouldn't I?

As we walked away Vernon asked "You'd like a cigarette now?"

Of course there was loss and heartache, crying and dreadful emptiness, allowing myself now to "let go" as I had not done through the eleven months of being strong for everyone. But when we went to visit John David on his first birthday a month later he looked well and bonny "in his rompers and pink jumper and new pink shoes" – he was being well cared for. Subsequent visits, sometimes by a series of tiring bus journeys, sometimes in a borrowed car, once memorably and most uncomfortably on Vernon's motorbike, always found him just as well looked after.

Let's leave him, for now at least, with my diary entry for the end of that first birthday:

"God, don't let me lose it all now. I kept it while I had to and now I still must for all our sakes, even if it no longer matters to Johnnie whether I go silly or not."

Now I was able to take a part time job as intended, once again cycling to and from the tube station, spending half days at the Belling Electric Company. A bonus of this was my ability to provide ourselves and other family members with top quality electric space heaters at cost price. Since our unheated houses relied heavily on this type of appliance for warmth I was quite popular, and returning from Canada many years later to stay with my parents I found my bedroom made cosy with one of their venerable "Bellings".

At about the same time we also acquired our hoped-for lodgers. An ex-WAAF friend Jean – one of the Winterton quartet – had married a Merchant Navy officer and they needed a base for three months while he took a course in London. So they and 20 month old Ann moved into the front half of our small house – one up and one down, sharing kitchen and bathroom as best we could. We managed well; it was good to have a baby around and our various schedules prevented us crowding each other unduly.

By November, when the Williamses had left and Vernon to his great relief had passed the first levels of his progression towards his I.E.E. certificate, I knew that the next baby would – should – be born very close to its elder brother's birthday the following May. Oddly I remember very little of that pregnancy. I continued to work for some months, briefly gave houseroom to a French student friend of my brother's, and was kept occupied managing my parents' mail, bills etc. during their three-month absence in South Africa. I do vividly remember meeting them at Victoria Station on their return in April 1950, amusing and alarming them by leaping, heavily pregnant, onto a luggage carrier the better to see them when the boat train pulled in.

During the first week of May Vernon was in bed with a heavy cold, and to pass the time we embarked on Tolstoy's War and Peace, taking turns to read aloud. By the 9th of May, his 30th birthday he was feeling better and ready to plan a celebration. Instead our early morning reading had to be abruptly halted. He, putting on a coat over pyjamas, ran to the public phone box at the corner to summon a taxi and I knocked on the neighbour's door to tell her we were on our way to the hospital. "I thought I heard you moving about the bedroom rather early" said an excited Mrs. Rees. So much for the insulation of pre-war semi-detached houses!

Up the long road, pink-blossom-lined once again, not this time to a private Nursing Home but to the local hospital. Only "at-risk" pregnancies were admitted to public hospitals in Britain at that time; home midwifery was efficient and commonly used and the well-to-do (or those with generous parents) went to private establishments. Due to John David's history I was this time eligible for hospital admission, much to Vernon's and our parents' relief.

Such a short and interesting morning that was! A group of students ringed the foot of my bed, notebooks in hand. We joked about the classroom atmosphere; I the specimen, Sister the teacher, they the class. A small shadow fell at one stage (though only in hindsight did I remember it as a shadow; at the time I accepted it as part of the routine). Sister leaned over me and said, "Mrs. Smith, I didn't think I would have to do an episiotomy, but I have decided that I will; baby is so anxious to come".

And come she did, Anna Mary, on the dot of 11 a.m. with the hospital's chief gynaecologist standing by to check her over and my mother 80 miles away on the end of a telephone waiting for his verdict –

a perfect baby!

Sure we had a few troubles and discomforts, she and I, the first few days. Some p.p.d. on my part and disagreement with mother over the names I had chosen, and on Mary's side a reluctance to properly nurse (remarkable considering how excellent an appetite she has maintained ever since). But when we went home and proudly paraded her in the big pram under the Willow Road cherry trees we were the ultimate besotted new parents. She was composed, contented, blonde and pretty. A letter from my father in reply to one of mine ended somewhat drily "I gather you are somewhat proud of her".

I have always thought that one of the strongest proofs of Vernon's life-long devotion to Mary was the willingness with which he shared his birthday. He could so easily have resented it – an only child, self-centred to a degree, accustomed to being celebrated on his own. But the two of them shared the 9th May with mutual enjoyment for the next 48 years.

To add to the glow of those early summer months of 1950, Vernon obtained a coveted post at The General Electric Company, some rungs up the ladder from his beginnings at the Standard Telephone labs. Unfortunately GEC was at Stanmore, inconveniently distant from Enfield for us in our then car-less days. Which is why and when the motorbike joined the family. Apprehension on everyone's part except for Vernon and Bill who respectively cherished and coveted it. In fact Vernon later sold the bike to Bill but he soon passed it on to another young friend – one set of parents' misgivings transferred to another!

Commuting thirty miles each way through suburban streets on a motor bike, in winter, was not pleasant. Increasingly we both knew it was time to move on; nearly three years in Willow Road had served their purpose. We spoke more frequently of emigrating – but to where? Australia in those days was so very far away. South Africa I rejected outright because of racial discrimination. The United States then, as now, was a magnet for the young and ambitious. Theo had sailed for the New World the previous year, and, returning for visits and exhibitions of his pictures, was full of praise. "Theo thinks America is bloody marvellous but he can't convince me". (Diary, 1951). Vernon would willingly have tried his fortunes there, but with Mary nearly a year old we had to turn our attention back to her. Healthy and charming still, she was without doubt very slow to develop. She was "late" to sit up, to crawl, and began to have disturbing spasms in which her head would drop to one side, her eyes cross, and her left arm and leg go limp.

Another visit was made to Dr. Sheldon; not this time to his private Harley Street office but in line at his Great Ormond Street Hospital clinic as humble National Health patients. Not that it made any difference to the quality of his concern and care. He kept Mary for three days of tests. When he returned her to us, himself pale and confused, he paced his office in genuine misery as he told us his findings. Somewhere, sometime, presumably at birth, she had sustained damage to the right hand side of her brain, the side controlling intellectual development and reasoning as well as the motor activity of the left side of her body. Into focus now swam that remembered image of Sister bending anxiously over me: "Mrs. Smith, I didn't think a cut would be necessary, but I find I must". Although it has never been and can never be proved that the resultant episiotomy caused Mary's brain damage, it is difficult to see what else it could have been.

However, continued Dr. S., she is teachable and will develop – she will simply be retarded. Take her home and raise her normally and you may well be surprised at her progress.

Or words to that effect. The only one that burned into our brains however was – retarded. A word I could not remember consciously using, in any context, ever before. Decades later it was to become politically incorrect to use it; all manner of vague euphemisms replaced it, but the bitter truth was, and is, that it defined Mary's life.

So – more sad news to pass on to others, some of whom found it hard to believe. "Surely" wrote Anne "you are being over-critical because of John David?". Nevertheless the loving support from families never failed us. How many grandparents can have been so sorely tried within the space of two years?

Even if dreams of emigration had to be shelved for a while, we did move in March of 1951. The village of Aldenham near Watford was easier travelling for Vernon (he motor-biked or bicycled to and from Stanmore in all weathers for the next 20 months) and altogether more pleasant than Enfield. With a loan from my father we bought another "semi" but as different as could be from cookie-cutter-type 106 Willow Road. This one was tucked away in a leafy quiet lane with only two or three near neighbours. It had a pretty garden and orchard behind, a garage, albeit a rather ramshackle one; a small greenhouse, to grandpa Jim Smith's delight; and at the back of the garage was a rare luxury in an age of one-bathroom houses – a separate loo.

Behind the orchard a field was home to sheep and rabbits, and once a year to a brief encampment of gypsies in traditional painted caravans. In front across the lane, another meadow, bordered by a row of tall old elm trees, stretched away to the spire of Aldenham church. I made friends, joined something called the Young Wives', sang in their choir and acted in their plays, and often walked across those fields to the home of my Aunt Ethel, one of mother's elder sisters, who was headmistress of a nearby village school.

We had many visitors, being within easy reach of London – and there was no long dull road up which to walk; the bus from Watford came to our corner! This was the pastoral village life in which I had grown up and I loved it. There was even Aldenham School, the same type and size of Sutton Valence, and the young chaplain and his wife became two of our closest friends.

But still restlessness gnawed at us both. England was moving only slowly, hesitantly and clumsily away from the effects of war; in fact the Korean war had begun. Winston Churchill's re-election as Prime Minister caused a brief surge of elation, but he was older, bereft now of his dramatic wartime stage – the magic was no longer there. At a personal level, we were still short of money and likely to remain so; things which many people considered basic like a telephone and a car were far beyond our reach. All our advancement hinged on Vernon's gaining his Professional Engineer's certificates. He was confident that he would, but the hours of study on top of the demands of a new job and the sorrows of Mary's handicaps were unrelentingly hard. Phrases began to recur – "a better life" – "I'm tired of everything being old or borrowed, I want NEW things". Plus a new thought taking root – is there a better future for Mary elsewhere? We took her to visit her big brother, thinking how unbearable it would be to have to place her also in an "institution". Johnnie was still well cared for, but – diminishing – somehow. Becoming a sorry little person to visit.

But we, and the world, moved on. In February 1952 King George VI died at the age of fifty seven; an early death caused, it was said, by the stresses of filling a role he had never expected, one forced on him by the abdication of his elder brother in 1937.

The necessary mourning was quickly succeeded by the excitement and glamour surrounding the new queen, the 27 year old second Elizabeth. The dramatic circumstances of her succession – her sudden return from a curtailed tour of Kenya "the slight, upright, black-clothed figure descending the aircraft steps, to be greeted with deep bows by her Prime Minister and half of his Cabinet" – this was history in the making. To a country so jaded, so starved of colour for dreary years, it was a re-awakening, a blessedly patriotic glow to warm a frosty winter and revive tired souls.

A family anecdote in this connection is worth re-telling here:

By a most memorable coincidence my brother Bill Bentley was in that place at that time. He was a 19 year old soldier doing his (then compulsory) two years of National Service in the armed forces and a 2nd Lieutenant in the regiment of the King's African Rifles. ("I wanted to see what a career in the Colonial Service might look like"). A group from his battalion had been detailed to provide sentry duties for Elizabeth and Phillip at Sagana Lodge, and Bill was the Guard Commander. They had planned a farewell party for the royal couple that evening, but instead, learning that they were in fact about to leave and return to England, he and his men hastily donned best uniforms and polished boots, formed up and presented arms; and thus it was that my brother gave the very first Royal Salute to our new Queen. Bill says: "Afterwards we went ahead with the party anyway, but it wasn't much of a bash".

Heady stuff for a young man only two years out of school!

In our private lives there were also happenings. Vernon achieved his A.M.I.E.E. at last, such a valuable spoke in his wheel and so hard-earned. My contribution to family success was to become safely pregnant, having had a miscarriage the previous year. On October 14th our second son was born at home. "Young Willie, our last hope" as Vernon dubbed him. He wasn't Willie, he was William James and not, as time would later tell, our last hope, but healthy and bonny and a joy to all. He was christened, not in the chapel of Sutton Valence School as John and Mary had been, but in the parish church at Aldenham by our new friend the school chaplain, David Wallace-Hadrill. A gathering of

IT'S ODD, THE THINGS ONE REMEMBERS

family and friends closely examined him, finding no fault. He flourished, was sunny and amiable, a beam of comfort in the demanding months to come.

Since the end of the war there had been increasing demand in North America for skilled British ex-servicemen, especially scientists and engineers, to work in the developing technical industries. We had known this of course; it had fuelled our interest in the possibility of emigrating. But the awareness came to our own doorstep when, a few months after Jamie's birth, two enthusiastic head-hunters, one American and one Canadian, came to G.E.C. and interviewed several people including Vernon. By November he received a firm offer of a post in the laboratories of the Canadian Westinghouse Company in Hamilton, Ontario.

In our previous discussions we had already agreed we did not want to live in the United States. (Vernon would have been more willing than I, but there was the possibility that Mary might not be admitted as an immigrant.) So, how about Canada, then? More familiar in some ways; it is still the Commonwealth after all! Robin Burns has settled in Toronto, not far from Hamilton; another GEC colleague recently went to Montreal to work for Bell Telephone – sure, why not Canada.

By the end of this eventful year of 1952 we had made our decision. We would take our few possessions, our lovely and flawed little girl and her equally lovely flawless brother, our optimistic and restless selves and we would head for the New World.

But now what a multitude of tasks lay ahead! What planning, what effort, what added anxieties for our long suffering parents, who rallied yet again to help us with this huge undertaking. Huge it seemed to me, only newly accustomed to caring for two babies – and how could we be so unfeeling as to remove so far this first grandchild in whom they could at last wholly rejoice? Said Eleanor Burns, Robin's Canadian wife, "I don't know how you can leave such a close and loving family as you have here in England".

True I was torn, yet for months I had been restless and certain that a new beginning was essential to us. For seven years we had struggled, as though on a hard, pebbly beach, with wearying post-war restrictions and impediments to progress, made harder by the shadows of John's and Mary's lives. The difficulties even began to nibble at the edges of the fabric of our marriage, and this neither of us was prepared to tolerate. Now, with Jamie flourishing, Mary manageable, and Vernon with his degree under his belt we had reached a stretch of smooth sand on that beach, and could summon the energy to move on.

The countdown began. The Aldenham house was sold and its contents either returned whence they had been borrowed or given to friends; only a few treasures and "good" household stuff were to go to Canada. Even that required hours of sorting, choosing and packing. I spent every available minute between baby chores – and so few minutes were left over from that never-ending cycle – stuffing packing cases, tea chests and our two battered tin trunks.

With Mary – Packing for Canada, 1953

IT'S ODD, THE THINGS ONE REMEMBERS

We had planned to spend our last Christmas with Vernon's parents in Sidmouth. Rail tickets were bought and bags packed but two mornings before departure Mary awoke covered in a rash – a full blown case of red measles. Bitter disappointment, but Vernon went anyway and his parents came a few weeks later to Sutton Valence to say their farewells and meet Jamie. (In retrospect I treasured most especially the sight of Grandpa Jim Smith holding that baby, because he was never able to meet his final grandson who was born nearly four years later, just five days after Jim's death).

Sutton Valence is where the children and I took refuge for the remaining two months. My sailing date was 29th February; Vernon was being flown out by his new employers and left in style on a BOAC Stratocruiser at the end of January. Brother Bill saw him off at Heathrow and reported "how jaunty and smart he looked with his new sports jacket and spiffy briefcase".

I, tying up loose ends of bank accounts, travel documents, health and ration cards, was vaguely unwell most of those last weeks, and so were the children – a legacy from Mary's measles, perhaps. But yet another reserve of emotional and physical energy had to be called up when we received a letter from the South Ockendon Hospital to say that Johnnie had died of pneumonia on 11th Febuary. The letter was addressed to Daddy since we had already given guardianship of John David to my parents. I had as yet no telephone number to reach Vernon and didn't want to send a telegram, so I scribbled a footnote on the back of the envelope of a letter already written and sealed.

Daddy and I drove, in foggy icy dark weather, across Kent and around London into flat grey Essex. While Daddy thawed out by the Matron's fire a young doctor took me to see Johnnie. I remember very little of the surroundings – I suppose it was a chapel – but they had laid him under a glass cover, white dress and cap and a rose in a vase by his head. It was comforting to see that such care had been taken but what greatly troubled me was that his eyes were not quite shut. I longed to reach over and close them but I could not because of the glass cover. They had left me alone with him, and I didn't afterwards think to ask anyone why he was so encased. I had seen him, that was mostly what mattered.

We drove home in the same bad weather, tired and thankful to safely arrive. Said Daddy along the way "You and I have done some strange things together haven't we my dear?"

This then was the All Clear for my going away. John David had released me from my guilt at leaving him; instead he went on by himself. (And, to our everlasting gratitude, with the compassionate help of the enlightened hospital staff who, knowing our circumstances, did not try to impede his journey.)

Moreover he had sent his brother – not to take his place but to succeed him.(Abridged diary entry):

> "Goodnight, John David. Wherever you are now you are richer than was your earthly self. The mercy of your death will overshadow the sorrow – which is the way it should be."

Meanwhile word had come from Vernon that he was being sent by Westinghouse to an Army Research Establishment near Quebec City, to be part of a group working on a 3-year contract with the Defence Research Board of Canada. (To do what, we would learn later). When you are a new boy you don't say no, I can't go, I have a family en route to Hamilton. So, he bought a second-hand 1947 Ford, put chains on its wheels and drove himself 800+ kilometres north through the snow, sending us instructions to follow. How vividly I remember Daddy methodically changing all the labels on our luggage from the Hamilton address to the new one Vernon had given us – that of a colleague in a suburb of Quebec City.

Since all would be so new anyway I wasn't dismayed by this change. Quebec would be an interesting part of Canada, one we might not

IT'S ODD, THE THINGS ONE REMEMBERS

have the opportunity to live in again. I spoke good French; it would be useful to have a chance to use it.

Let go then, and let's go.

On 28th February Daddy and Bill, Mary, James and I and my seven pieces of luggage set out for Liverpool. Mother left the school where she was teaching to come to Maidstone East station to say her goodbyes. Tense and difficult minutes sitting in the train while it waited in the siding; the same one whence we had so often left, separately or all together, on so many journeys. I have never been able to remember what words we exchanged, only an acute awareness of how much she was holding in – how that famous self-control of hers was working overtime.

Cameos of the next twenty-four hours:
- A cup of tea in the restaurant at Euston station with poor baby red-faced and over hot in his carry-bed because I had piled all his bedding on top, that being the easiest way to carry it!:
- Mary, restless, clambering over cases and under tables; my thankfulness at having Bill to carry her:
- Difficult night in a Liverpool hotel; central heating too high, babies (and adults) unaccustomed:
- Dockside in a huge shed for the paperwork and luggage check. And there was the S.S. SAMARIA looming over us.
- Relief at being assured that visitors were allowed on board because since the war this had not always been the case:
- And , as a final homage to British bureaucracy, I handed over our food ration books to an official at the foot of the gangway!

We found my cabin, way, way down. Daddy, eyes on the ball for what mattered most, tracked down my stewardess and steward, charmed them and paved the way for my comfort. (Anne Worthington, the stewardess, proved to be a friend indeed and in need on that voyage. She visited us in our new home later in the summer when the ship docked again in Quebec.) Daddy handed me a small book, a present from mama. That gave a lift, as did the flowers and telegrams which greeted me in the cabin. "Just like in the films" said Bill.

Leaving Mary in Anne W's care I carried James up onto the windy deck. Daddy and Bill sprinted down the gangway, off and away – running and waving, running for their train – scarves and open coats flying, laughing, and waving ....

And I standing disembodied between the two worlds; my new son in my arms, my father and brother disappearing back onto the English shore.

The S.S.Samaria

PART II – WEST OF THE ATLANTIC

CHAPTER 5

QUEBEC AND ONTARIO

Quebec, 1955

We left Liverpool on the 29th of February 1953 and docked in Halifax on the 9th of March. The voyage was of course a great adventure, but it was quite a difficult one. Weary after the busy and emotional preceding weeks, and dealing with the needs of two infants in cramped and unfamiliar surroundings, I was not feeling particularly well (I developed a badly infected thumb and Mary, to my dismay, "came out in spots" – a residual infection from her measles of the previous Christmas, I suppose.). But there was support and friendliness all along the way: camaraderie among others in the laundry room (and what a relief to discover that amenity! I had not yet reached the world of disposable diapers); and the always helpful Anne who minded the baby while the toddler and I navigated steep gangways to the dining room and outer decks.

When on 9th March we docked in Halifax I wondered how I would deal with disembarkation, customs, those seven pieces of luggage, and finding my train to Quebec. But on Pier 21 all was organised and help again forthcoming; first from the Red Cross nursery staff who relieved me of two weary children while I dealt with the necessary formalities. Second, and most memorable, the cheerful platoon of Canadian infantry assembled on the railway platform whose sergeant I approached, almost in desperation, to ask if they would help me. Like service people in transit anywhere, they were only too pleased to have something useful to do, and in no time we three were established in our seats and the luggage safely stowed in the freight car. The sergeant even came by later to see if we needed anything, and for the rest of the 36 hour journey a kind steward looked after us.

SS Samaria is a big part of our family history, the link between my old and new lives. To revisit Pier 21 over fifty years later was a moving experience as it must be for so many Canadians, and I salute the people who created this "living museum".

The railway station at which we arrived is at Levis, opposite Quebec City on the south shore of the St. Lawrence river. There our train made the last of its many, many stops since Halifax and there, as I bundled up bags and babies, appeared Vernon, threading his way through the crowded carriage.

The huge thankfulness of that meeting! He scooped Mary up over his shoulder, (a small red shoe dropping off to be scrambled for under the seat), and out we all went to the station yard. There sat a blue car, ours, our first-ever car, the second-hand 1947 Ford which Vernon had bought two weeks previously in Hamilton. Even in that mentally-crowded moment I recalled his plaint from the last months in England: "I am tired of old things and making do; I want NEW things." The car may not have been new but to us it seemed to symbolize the new beginnings.

So the four of us drove proudly onto the ferry and across the wide grey ice-studded river. Nearing the city, its famous Heights crowned

IT'S ODD, THE THINGS ONE REMEMBERS

by the Citadel to the left and the old houses of lower town clambering steeply to the Dufferin Terrace and the sprawling stone pile of the Chateau Frontenac Hotel – familiar from history and tourist literature and to become even more familiar over the next two and a half years as home. Disembarking, bundling again into our fine blue car, we climbed the steep winding streets, I marvelling at the brilliance of the white deep snow and the blue clear sky. The temperature that first day was -10C, which I was to discover is quite balmy for Quebec City.

Settled into a comfortable suite at the Laurier Hotel on Grande Allée, with babies at last comfortably spread out on huge double beds, Vernon told of the apartment he had rented, which was ready for occupation except that "the painters need to know what colours you would like; then we can move in a few days". So, within hours of my journey's end I was discussing by telephone, in French, with an Italian painter, the décor of my new home!

As at every stage of my travels the pressing needs of infants took precedence and left little room for homesickness or uncertainty. Now, the immediate test was to find a supply of the right dried milk food for James. (I had yet to learn, with the rest of my large new vocabulary, to call it "baby formula"). So after dark Vernon and I set out in search of a *pharmacie* that might be open. The one we found, with a corner entrance on one of the steep side streets off Grande Allée, remains one of my most vivid memories of those first confusing days. It took some minutes to make my request clear, but with huge relief we did find nothing less than "Cow and Gate" – the Rolls Royce of British infant food and with which baby was already familiar.

Rue St. Jean Bosco was in early 1953 a muddy lane leading off the Ste. Foy road to the west of the city. Two new four storey apartment blocks – and very little other building – had recently been completed and on the ground floor of one of these we made our first Canadian home – a bright two bedroom flat with a tiny balcony. The other occupants were mostly newcomers also, both service people and civilians; many like

Vernon were travelling daily to the Army base at nearby Valcartier . It was there that the project was being carried out to which he had been assigned.

The reason Vernon had, on his arrival in Hamilton, been so abruptly and unexpectedly sent on to Quebec was that the Canadian Westinghouse laboratories had just been commissioned to build the radar guidance unit for an air-to-air missile which had been designed by the Defence Research Establishment at Valcartier. This was Velvet Glove, the first of a series of imaginatively named weapons developed over the next three years. Production had just begun in early 1953 so the team assembled at DREV(Defence Research Board Establishment Valcartier) was a new and enthusiastic mixture of military and civilian, scientists, engineers and technicians, French-speaking and English-speaking – a small but strong proportion of them being the new British émigrés.

So we had in many ways an easier path than many immigrants. Not only a job guaranteed and waiting (Vernon used to say, with only a bit of poetic licence, that he left General Electric in Stanmore on Friday and started at Westinghouse on Monday) but one which placed us at once among people of like minds and in a small community which for the time being was working towards one objective. Friends were quickly made, useful baby-sitting hours exchanged; the more permanent Valcartier personnel who lived in Quebec or its western suburbs of Sillery and Ste. Foy invited us to their homes.

There began some long and deep friendships which were to take us on to Ottawa, Washington and back to Ottawa again and to endure for decades. There were Robin and Adrian Duguid, two bright and committed Anglophones, he had been a Rhodes Scholar at Oxford; Margaret and Gordon Watson, he becoming years later, in Vernon's words "the best boss I ever had". Jean and Bill Bates, who with two year old Vicky had actually crossed on the Samaria with me but we had not met (they had decided that emigration warranted a first class passage!) – Margaret and Farrell Chown, whose youngest became one of my godsons; Dick and Johanna Cox – she very German and he very quietly English, they decided after a year that Canada was not for them and returned to Sevenoaks in Kent, where I used to visit them and was honoured by being made yet again a godmother to their daughter Elisabeth. And of course Margaret and Douglas Crombie who 53 years later are with me still. Resolute transplanted Scots, they soon found the sport of curling was alive and well in Canada but made sure we all knew its true origins.

Everything needed doing at once! Baby James in his snug carry-cot was the only member of the family with a bed. Leaving him in the care of a kind Navy wife across the hall we headed to Lower Town and the second-hand furniture stores. Within a day or two we had collected two iron bedsteads, a heavy old-fashioned iron crib for Mary; kitchen table, chairs, a high chair, and stove and refrigerator of such dated models that outspoken Robin Duguid pronounced them "downright unsafe". Two solid, ugly chests of drawers; Vernon painted them and all the iron beds a cheerful blue and they remained in the childrens' bedrooms for many years.

Now how was I, who had not yet learned to drive a car, to get around with two infants in tow? The handsome impractical English perambulator had been left behind for another General Electric Company baby, so in its place we bought, again second-hand, a compact folding baby carriage for walking to the corner store and a very light stroller to take with Mary on the buses. (I referred to it as a "push chair" until, met with blank looks, I learned the correct word.)

All this Vernon and I did together. I don't remember how much time he took from work, perhaps a week, but it must have been a double effort for him, barely into a new job in a new country, to divide his time between that and the hundred domestic details. The fact that several colleagues, newly arrived like ourselves, were in the same situation, helped of course. But it was characteristic of him to be totally supportive in practical matters, most competent in all our household moves; making them easier in every way for me.

In his work, Vernon was in his element and soon, deservedly, absorbed therein. Once we were settled domestically he was much away from home. So, though the neighbours were friendly and congenial, though our social life was lively and I was quickly learning to appreciate Canada, I now had hours enough alone to feel spells of real homesickness for England. I felt that if only I could just take the children to show their bereft grandparents that they were indeed thriving, that I was indeed committed to my new life – that "if only" I could just set foot in England to remind myself it was still there ... but it was out of the question. There were no plentiful discount air fares, or charters, or a choice of competitive airlines offering short-stay packages; there simply was not the money to fly and it would be totally impractical – maybe dangerous? – to embark on a reverse sea voyage so soon. I could only rely, as I had done all my life because so much of it had been spent away from family, on long and frequent letters and on sending a regular supply of Vernon's excellent photographs. When in 1954 he was himself able to go to England in connection with work, I was in equal parts envious and thankful. He took with him tape recordings of the family, and of course more photos, visited both sets of parents and reported back to me that he left them well reassured that we were safe, healthy, befriended – that Canada was not a colonial backwater but a lively, burgeoning country full of interest and possibilities.

A far more serious result of this loneliness was that I drifted into an affair which lasted from April to September 1955, when we left Quebec. I was extraordinarily naïve, but such was Vernon's absorption in his work and travel, and when at home in only practical and mechanical matters, that I convinced myself that he wasn't interested in any activities of mine. Naïve indeed. When in an effort to clear my conscience I told him about this episode he was of course devastated, and I in turn shattered by the extent of his devastation. It was a tribute to the strength of our marriage, and of Vernon's maturity relative to my own foolish lack of judgement, that we survived this. We did; we moved on together to the successes and satisfactions of the next job,

IT'S ODD, THE THINGS ONE REMEMBERS

the next home and the next baby, past the adjustments of immigration to the establishment of our permanent life in Canada.

But of course it could never be erased. It exacerbated a latent jealousy in Vernon's nature and so clouded some friendships, put constraints on my own working years – "Just who is that fellow who runs your office?" – and explained, to ourselves if not to anyone else, the sometimes undercurrent of strains in our daily lives. However, in our later years together it had faded, become part of our long shared past. Perhaps by my care of Vernon over his last ten years I was able to expiate that folly; certainly his often expressed appreciation was unequivocal.

No good marriage should ever be subjected to such a test – how sad it is that many are – always have been and always will be.

Through all this – what of the children? baby James was a joy, a balm, a delight. In spite of many disruptions to what should normally have been the quiet routine of a 6-monther, his disposition was sunny and amiable and, as he grew able to play with her, a bright foil to Mary's ponderous ways and a stimulus to her.

So now we needed to address Mary's needs – her development and her education, if any. We knew that in Montreal at that time was Dr. Wilfrid Sheldon, a brain specialist famous far outside Canada. We arranged to have one of his assistants, Preston Robb, examine Mary. (A big adventure, travelling to Montreal and staying overnight with ex G.E.C. friends who had come to Canada just ahead of us). Said Dr. Robb, don't fret. "Don't worry about an 'education' – her little brother is the best teacher she could presently have and your loving home her best foundation. She will be educable yes, but there is plenty of time for that."

Encouraging in the short term, but still it was becoming clear to us that once the Velvet Glove contract was completed a move to Ontario would better concentrate our lives, domestically as well as career-wise. Any "work" I could do would have to be on a volunteer basis, so what more appropriate than to combine that with whatever facilities were available for Mary? It was now the end of 1954 and the new year brought bitter weather. The novelty of our first winter – deep snow drifts, sub-zero temperatures, driving with chains on the car wheels – had worn off. The children caught influenza which in Mary's case set off frightening convulsions, the first of periodic *petit mal* seizures which were to recur over the next three years until the right balance of medication was found.

Quebec, in short, was losing its appeal, or to be fair its initial attraction as our first base in Canada. Though we had both formed a great attachment to its landscapes, its history and culture, and to its people whose lives embodies those things. It was not chance that brought us back to "the Quebec side" when a few years later, looking for a summer getaway we found our beloved Blue Sea Lake deep in the Gatineau hills, which fifty years on is still my first refuge. There will be more about Blue Sea Lake later.

So in October 1955 Vernon returned to the Canadian Westinghouse Laboratories. in Hamilton. Entrusted with the task of find us a home, I proudly chose our very first "owned" house, a 1 ½ storey cottage on a brand new estate in Dundas, which in those days was still a picturesque small town tucked under the western end of the escarpment known as Hamilton Mountain. The home cost $11,500 but it had four tiny bedrooms, 2 up and 2 down – no garden, no hedge or fence – a sea of mud in wet weather and blowing sand in the dry; a patch of reluctant grass in front. Vernon painted the kitchen bright red, one bedroom yellow, another pale green. And he bought me a car! A fragile second-hand Austin, soon christened Bouncer, with manual transmission and a horn with a tendency to stick at embarrassing times. I needed a car, because we found that in Hamilton there was a small school for mentally retarded children (no lengthy vague euphemisms in those days) – one of the first in the province. There Mary was enrolled. A bus collected and returned her to a point outside town to which I drove Bouncer twice daily with James bundled in the back. No car seats, yet.

IT'S ODD, THE THINGS ONE REMEMBERS

Dundas, 1956 - Our first 'own' house

In 1956, three and a half years after we parted on Maidstone East station, my mother came to stay.

She had planned to visit first a sister in Philadelphia, but for me to know that she was this side of the ocean yet not with me was more than I could endure. With some trepidation (Aunt Lena was after all a Banks Girl, accustomed to doing things her way) I asked if mama could come to us first. Both agreed, and Vernon and I drove to New York to meet her. She had expected of course to see Lena, and the expression on her face when she realised who we were was almost worth the separation of those years. (She had suffered, but recovered from, a nervous breakdown in 1953-54 which had added weight to my own load of guilt at taking my family away from her). On embracing us – "Now I shall cry" – she said; something she prided herself in never doing. We stayed overnight in New York; Vernon took happy photographs of M and me walking the streets – then back to the little Dundas house and the babies – and so much family news to exchange!

From mother I needed to hear all details of my brother Bill's wedding in early 1958 to Adele Patricia Berry, my new sister-in-law. My dear Pat, who over sixty years has so enriched our family and become to me such a dear and close friend that we refer to each other as "the sister I never had".

Bill met her in Oxford where he was at Exeter College pursuing his studies (and becoming an enthusiastic and valuable member of the college Rowing Eight); Pat was taking Nursing Training at the Radcliffe College. But her home was on the western edge of the English Lake District, a region familiar to us all, especially Bill and my father, through many school holidays spent walking and climbing there. Visits were made to both her widowed mother and to our parents – my father, instantly enchanted; my mother characteristically more analytical and cautious! – but of course she came to love Pat as did we all. To mourn with her at the loss of her first baby, Mark, at the age of a few weeks – (as so deeply did I! Remembering John David, right there was the first strong bond between us) – to cherish the four very healthy children who followed him – above all to appreciate her devotion to Bill through the rigours and challenges of life as a "Shell International wife". This meant creating, with varying degrees of help or hindrances, a comfortable home in countries and continents from Ghana to Hong Kong to Saigon to Japan over the next forty years. Dealing with tact and charm a procession of foreign and homegrown VIPs; the while juggling the different schooling needs of the children, often requiring that Pat return with them to England for periods of time. The most dramatic of these being a hasty departure from Saigon at the time of the Viet Nam war with the USA.

In retirement Pat and Bill settled in a beautiful corner of the beloved Lake District but Pat embarked on a new career, that of breeding and raising alpacas! She had fallen in love with these animals on a visit to Peru and remarked that their grazing there was similar to her own rolling grassy fields in Cumbria; maybe they would thrive there? She came home and bought her first alpaca, established a varied herd which eventually numbered over two hundred; toiled and learned and became for the next 20 years or more a respected leader and mentor among others all over Britain involved in this very challenging work.

She was a founding member of the British Alpaca Society and is a former chairman. The alpacas are now gone, but with Pat and Bill as its welcoming and generous heart, Syke House near Penrith remains a well-loved magnet and refuge for a procession of relations, friends and hangers-on; not least myself. (It has become a family joke that of recent years I have made my Positively Last Visit to England quite frequently – I believe it is five times at the last count).

To return to Mama's and my "catching-up" session; I was able to tell her that by Christmas she would have another grandchild. Our careful pattern of two-year intervals between children had been disrupted by the emigration and the anxieties and adjustments which followed it, but four years was not so bad and we were very pleased with ourselves. Even more pleased – overjoyed, thankful and blessed were we, when David Mark, our first native Canadian was born at 1 a.m. on December 20th 1956. He was probably helped on his way by the bumpy drive in Bouncer up Hamilton Mountain to the hospital. He came healthy and perfect like his brother but to develop a very different character. Neither this nor the four year age gap prevented them from becoming loyal companions in a household which gave them more than their fair share of challenges.

The date of David's birth made it especially significant for his grandmother Lilian Smith. Vernon's father, Jim, had died just five days before. With the baby's arrival so imminent she generously agreed that Vernon should not go to England to be with her, but she was lovingly supported by family there. Maybe, we thought, the child will come on grandpa Jim's birthday, the 21st. He missed it by a day, but no grandmother who had suffered with us through two flawed births could do anything but rejoice at his health and safety. The following year Lilian sailed to Canada and spent a happy summer acquainting with him and the two toddlers who she had last seen as babies. Not incidentally, being an invaluable help to Vernon and me.

In the eighteen months since his return to Canadian Westinghouse Vernon had become less satisfied with his work. All his experience had been in or closely involved with laboratories, but now he was increasingly required to deal with administration and sales matters. Frustration – "They aren't going to make a salesman out of me!" – prompted an enquiry to Gordon Watson at the Defence Research Board of Canada with whom Vernon had worked well in Quebec. The reply was prompt and satisfactory; "We would be very pleased to see you". He was interviewed for and accepted, initially, a position in the Weapons Research Division of DRB. With variations in departments, responsibility, rank and physical relocations, his working life was established for the next 25 years, a period which fairly paralleled the life of the Defence Research Board itself. The Board was a dynamic place and Vernon was lucky to be there during its best years. It was the foreshadowing of its demise and the disillusionment therefore among so many bright and dedicated minds which prompted Vernon's early retirement at the age of fifty four.

But that is not now. Now is Vernon setting off once again ahead of us to a new job and to find a new house in Ottawa. Both came easily, the work because it was just what he wanted and the house through help of a colleague. "Come and have a look at mine! They are building a new development and there is one just like it down the street".

Indeed there was, a 4-bedroom box of a house twice the size of my first find in Dundas; an appropriate family home such as were springing up in subdivisions all around the city – all around most cities in the country. We bought it, and the helpful colleague and his family became neighbours and close friends. We found we had much in common with Prue and Jim Irvine. We had all been in the RAF or RCAF, we had all worked in Radar. They had four children to our three and when they added a fifth she became another in my growing "family" of godchildren. When we left Washington at the end of our 3-year posting in 1966 Jim found he was to be sent there also; what more convenient and acceptable than to take over the rental of our house there!

IT'S ODD, THE THINGS ONE REMEMBERS

Again, I move ahead too fast. In 1957 Copeland Park on the (then) western edge of Ottawa was becoming occupied with similar young families sharing the concerns of settling in. We started a Babysitters' Club, trading and accumulating hours; a commuting car pool for Vernon and Jim plus two others enabled the wives to share driving also (though I was lucky to have Bouncer for a while longer).

Vernon with his usual care and thoroughness had already made enquiries about possible schooling for Mary. He was put in touch with Toddy Kehoe, a remarkable woman who had, a few years previously, launched the small group which became the Ottawa and District Association for Retarded Children. Although I can't claim to have been a founding member, I am 60 years later one of the longest surviving ones and have a drawer full of nicely worded plaques and certificates to that effect. Now, clumsily but with political correctness, called the Ottawa-Carleton Association for Persons with Developmental Disabilities, this large, provincially funded, somewhat bureaucratic organisation bears little resemblance to that early band of parents. We knew what we needed but were breaking new ground. It was not until the early 1960s, when John Kennedy, himself the brother of a mentally handicapped woman, became President of the United States and his family spearheaded increasing awareness of, and generous funding for, the education of such children, that real progress began in North America. The history of that progress is inevitably woven into our own family history. Mary's presence marked all our lives; the necessity was paramount that she not dominate them, most especially the lives of Jim and David.

Mrs. Kehoe had as yet no school, just a classroom set aside at the old Kent Street Public School. There Mary, aged seven, spent a few hours each day. About the same time Jim began kindergarten at Woodroffe Public School. On the first day I left him sitting cross-legged on the floor, staring at me tearful and reproachful as I beat my retreat. Those first years of his early school life were plagued with nervous apprehension. But I think his innate love of learning came soon enough to his rescue. When David in his turn began school a few years later things came easier to him; less introspective, with a more in-your-face look to the world, he breezed along. They were both "constructive" – with Vernon's interest and input there were always several school projects spread about the floor.

So at last we felt we were leading a Normal Family Life. That such a stage should be reached only after seven years of marriage seems strange, but they had been an obstacle course , those years. We marvelled at our apparent serenity. I so exactly remember it; sitting in that newly built, sparsely furnished house smiling at each other and saying – things seem to be going right!

All in all, they did. But for that very reason this ceases to be my story and becomes my family's, which makes it very much more difficult to write. Will Jim and David remember the times and happenings as I relate them or will all this seem like a fiction to them? Can I possibly do them and Vernon justice?

Given the difference in Vernon's and my characters I feel that he was a more powerful influence on them in their growing-up years, and that I took a back seat. Maybe my input was absorbed at a quieter level ... in any case I still say that they raised themselves in spite of us. I never presume to say "I am proud of my sons" because to have pride implies that they are my achievements. Instead I do say with all my heart that I am enormously, ceaselessly proud to be related to them. Their successes are theirs.

A digression, but I totally mean this. It had to be recorded.

1958 was an eventful year; first because Vernon, myself, Mary and Jim, having lived in Canada for the requisite five years, all now qualified for Canadian Citizenship. In a brief visit to Ottawa City Hall we proudly received our Certificates, telling us that we are " entitled to all the rights and privileges and subject to all the responsibilities, obligations and duties of a Canadian Citizen." The rights and privileges we have all certainly and gratefully enjoyed. As for the responsibilities,

IT'S ODD, THE THINGS ONE REMEMBERS

obligations and duties, I can only hope that according to our varied abilities the four of us have done our best to fulfil them.

In late summer we returned for the first time to England. A great undertaking, a great joy, an accumulation of vivid impressions and happy reunions. I flew alone with the three children, juggling meal trays for Mary and Jim with a squirming 20 month old David on my lap. Solving sleeping arrangements by letting Jim lie on the floor under the seat in front, Mary stretched across a friendly lady neighbour's arm. Me – I was bruised and stiff for several days from holding that bouncing, not very sleepy baby, but all was compensated for by seeing Daddy and a dear family friend at the airport. Thinking kindly to break the drive from Heathrow to Sutton Valence they had packed a lunch, and detoured to Hampton Court Palace to picnic in the grounds! Alas, we were all too tired to much enjoy it; Mary lay down and promptly fell asleep on the grass, and I just wanted to see Mother who had stayed home to be ready for our arrival. Typically efficient, she had hired a local girl to stay with us for the six weeks. Hazel became a friend and a blessing, especially when later we took train to Sidmouth to spend time with Vernon's mother.

England! Surprised at how much I had forgotten. How small the distances; how tidy the paved footpaths, how ablaze with colour even the smallest flower-filled gardens. We had warm weather, warm welcomes everywhere. Vernon, who had been in Europe at NATO meetings, was able to join us towards the end and, thank goodness, to fly home with us. How much easier was that voyage.

*Return visit to England 1958 – in the garden of
my parents' house at Sutton Valence School*

The eventfulness of this year 1958 concluded with its most significant one. In November two months after our return, Mary was admitted to a Hospital School at the town of Smith's Falls, 40 miles south of Ottawa. I had heard of this establishment in my search for schooling for Mary; I had met the parents of a boy who was living there. Joan W. had asked me quietly one day, "have you thought of Smiths Falls for Mary?". All I could see in my mind was an image of the South Ockendon Hospital where John David had gone and my immediate response was a horrified No. Gently it was pointed out to me that this was a hospital school and that the school component had a good reputation. Would I not go with Joan next time she visited Frankie? Before we left for England I did so, and came home to tell Vernon what I had learned. We submitted an application for Mary and she was accepted for admission after our return to Canada.

We knew that something had to be done. As the boys neared school age they needed an easier atmosphere at home; so frequently were their activities and concentration disrupted by Mary's eccentric behaviour.

IT'S ODD, THE THINGS ONE REMEMBERS

Her petit mal seizures were still not under control and I did not think that the medical attention she was receiving was adequate; in every way we needed more professional advice and care for her.

So while staying at S.V. we made a point of taking her round the dormitories and the common rooms, talking to chosen of the boys who quickly picked up on the situation: "See Mary, when you go back to Canada you could go to a boarding school like this! We like it here."

So she did. Thus, instead of leaving an unknowing blind baby to the care of others as I had done nine years previously, I now handed over a cheerful, pretty, chatty eight-year-old to whom the interviewing Matron exclaimed, I think you will be really happy here, Mary!

And mostly she was.

When the hospital school finally closed its doors 51 years later several people wrote their appreciation to the local newspaper. My letter was headlined "My daughter blossomed at Rideau". (The facility had at some stage been re-christened The Rideau Regional Hospital School). Mary learned to read and write and spell; she developed an interest in the Anglican church, its hymns and form of service, and was confirmed therein by a remarkable young chaplain. She was continually being tried and assessed in a variety of skills; laundry (yes, very good), sewing (no), mail delivery, dining room care, and of course singing, with her inherited good musical ear. When she was 21 she was among the first group of residents to be moved to group homes in the community – the outside world. Over time she had to adjust to several moves as the politics and finances of the system fluctuated, but always she came home to us for family rituals, holidays, birthdays.

As I write this very incomplete summary of Mary's life so far she is 62 years old and living "semi-independently" in her own spacious flat but with resident supervision. She is increasingly lame, physically slow, medicated, with a rated IQ steady at 50. But as she always has been she remains meticulously tidy, highly articulate, definite of opinions and preferences and above all rooted in her family. Attempts to encourage friendships and activities among her colleagues are mostly rebutted: "They are OK but they are not my family".

A tribute no doubt to our support, but a heavy weight for a family so small in number – and so increasingly old. Withal, she would remain the binding thread between the other four of us as our family life continued to develop.

Develop it certainly did, over the next five years before another move took us temporarily away from Ottawa. In 1960 both my parents came to stay. The success of my mother's 1956 visit emboldened cautious Norman to venture on the long sea voyage; less expensive (and probably to him less hazardous) than the airborne one. It was a great joy to me to be able to show them both that our Canadian life was settling on solid ground; to introduce them to friends and our favourite places, to novelties like shopping malls (anathema to my father) and most especially to our newly discovered treasure, the beautiful Blue Sea Lake in Quebec.

These recent reunions, and a further short trip to England in 1962 when Vernon and I, en route to a holiday in Europe, deposited the boys upon their grandparents' doorstep for two weeks, helped to close the gulf of separation caused by our emigration. I felt cautiously that it was just possible we might be again that happy family in which I had grown up; a changed, older family but one whose cohesion was vital to me.

In 1962 personal affairs were put aside as Canada became reluctantly but inevitably involved in the so-called "Cold War", beginning with the anxious days in October when U.S. President John Kennedy revealed that there were Soviet ballistic missiles being stockpiled in Cuba with the capability to hit North America. As the crisis escalated the Americans urgently demanded that Canada place our military on alert and take part in a shared defence of the continent. Although Prime Minister Diefenbaker stalled initially, and the Defence Department sidetracked the issue by "days of needless debate", Canadian forces were eventually placed on a READY state of military vigilance. Leave for the Forces was cancelled and units were brought up to wartime strength.

At DRB Headquarters, as elsewhere, contingency plans were made and Vernon was spending very long hours there. One day he explained to me that if I should receive a certain coded telephone call from him I was to pack some essentials, drive with the children to Blue Sea Lake and rent a cabin there. In other words, get away from Ottawa. However, as history has well recorded, the short-lived threat of nuclear war was averted, and Kennedy's stand-off against the Soviets is still considered a highlight of his administration.

Nevertheless the Canadian Defence Department was heavily criticized for its vacillation, and there followed some reorganisation of its Washington headquarters, including the Defence Research Board component. At the end of the year Vernon was told to expect a date for his posting there. Excitement! The three-year tours of duty in Washington were coveted plums. In England my Uncle Byrne Derrick averred "Not just anyone is sent to Washington". We were given a farewell party, began plans to sell the house, when suddenly the posting date was deferred – "at least until the New Year".

In fact it was not until August 1963 that we finally waved goodbye to the very large furniture van as it moved away down Erindale Drive. There had been a second farewell party with, rather generously under the circumstances, a second nice gift!; we did sell the house; we visited Mary and ensured that she was well cared for and content, promising to bring her to Washington twice a year for holidays. Goodbye to friends and neighbours of seven years, and to the boys' first school.

Goodbye to Ottawa – 1963

Vernon and I had been on a house-hunting visit and chosen one in a quiet corner of Arlington, Virginia – "the other side of the Potomac". A solid 3-storey red-brick in the popular Colonial style, with a garden that backed onto woods sloping down to a creek which flowed in turn into the great river. This we hoped would be a bonus for two still small boys as they coped with many challenges in a new world.

Challenges for all of us. Not least for Vernon, who would need to strengthen some of his weaker character traits – tact, patience, diplomacy! – among American colleagues still wary of Canada's commitment to their policies. For myself, I don't remember being apprehensive; in fact I welcomed the possibility of taking more part in Vernon's professional life, of being useful therein. The social obligations I knew I could handle, and I would have the support of at least two wives of senior colleagues who were already good friends.

Into the car then, fully loaded, and farewell to Ottawa on a hot summer day, only to learn how very much hotter it would be at the end of our journey. (One car, with one cat, but when we returned three years later what a caravan we were! One large car hauling a small trailer and containing a driver, a boy, and one or two cats. One large car hauling a motor boat and containing a driver, a boy and a bird in a cage. Which shows that we acquired things in that time.)

IT'S ODD, THE THINGS ONE REMEMBERS

What else did we acquire? For all of us, a new view of the world, at least as seen through North American eyes. For Jim and David especially, three years of profound social and educational change broadened their horizons, and maybe helped to give them the confidence to choose their own paths when the time came.

CHAPTER 6

VIRGINIA AND MEXICO

Did I say it was hot? The earliest memory which we all share is of our brief stay at the Key Bridge Marriott Hotel while we waited for our furniture to arrive, where we spent as much time as possible in the swimming pool. We tried some sightseeing – Jim as always willing and eager for that – but I remember mostly my hesitation in so much as opening the car door, knowing that I would be instantly blanketed by the outside heat.

Rivercrest is an enclave of a half dozen winding streets sloping uphill from our aforementioned woods to the Military Road. Substantial late 1950s homes inhabited by substantial middle class white families with a variety of professions and occupations. It was not a community in the social sense; there were no organised activities for children, no playground, baseball court or football field. They played in each others' homes or on the relatively safe and quiet streets; some went with their parents to The Club, or away to exclusive summer camps. We made friends with one next-door family and got on well enough with the other, but our closest friends in our new neighbourhood were two English families who were there as employees of the World Bank in Washington. (Thus foreshadowing the course of Jim Smith's professional life, but that will be his story, not mine.)

The house sprawled over two levels with the garage and garden doors below opening onto a small patch of lawn bordering the woods. There was also a side door leading off Vernon's study onto a bare concrete patio railed by iron fencing. It must have been intended for a barbeque or sitting-out place but, facing south and west with no awning or overhang, it was perpetually far too hot to be of any use.

Our modest amount of furniture was rather swallowed up by the large handsome rooms. We had brought from England to Canada only three small antique pieces, and since then accumulated only what was needed as the family grew. Vernon enjoyed making things and had built shelving, bookcases, cabinets; all very neat and sturdy and meticulously finished in arborite, an enduring material now probably extinct but with a wood-like sheen which never needed polishing. These were utilitarian rather than decorative, but we scattered them, our few tables, beds, dressers and chairs as best we could. Compensating with one extravagance in the form of lovely new fibreglass curtains for all the many windows, in my favourite shades of turquoise, green and white. A good investment, they gave a classy grace to the windows of three more homes back in Canada and lasted another 20 years.

It was now necessary to find some help with cleaning this place – I must, like everyone else, employ a maid. The owners of the house were a military family presently on a tour of duty in the Pacific islands. Their Arlington home was Mrs. W's pride, and she had left me a binder with neat lists of products and the appropriate places to use them. A special cleaner for the slates in the front hall and another for the kitchen floor; a special soft brush for the brocade wall covering in the dining room and another for the chandelier! Her own help was unavailable, but she must have left me a recommendation and a telephone number because somehow Mrs. Ella Byrd came into our lives. A slight middle-aged lady, quiet and dignified, she travelled out twice a month from north east Washington by bus, and between us we kept order, as near to Mrs. W's instructions as we could.

IT'S ODD, THE THINGS ONE REMEMBERS

David's first meeting with Mrs. Byrd was an epiphany for him. In 1963 Canada was not, as it is now, home to thousands of immigrants from Africa and the Far East; certainly there had been none in our corner of west-end Ottawa. "Oh" he said. "Hello. Don't you ever wash your face?". She laughingly forestalled my hasty attempt at explanation and said to David "Why honey, I jes guess you have never seen no negro person in yo lil life, have yo?".

I always called her Mrs. Byrd and made sure that the family did also. She was bewildered – "Why Ma'am, my other ladies, they all call me Ella". But "you call me Mrs. Smith," I said, "and you are a lady a bit older than I , so you are Mrs. Byrd."

Near the end of our three years together she invited me, with trepidation but quiet dignity, to "do her the honour" of visiting her at home. I found her in her small immaculate apartment, where she gave me a cup of tea and the gift of a smart black clutch purse which I treasured for years.

Not the common relationship in those parts, in those times, between white mistress and black maid. I did have to make some concessions to the different culture in which I was now living; I learnt quickly to keep my mouth shut on many subjects from the Viet Nam war to "communists" to segregation – but I could not accept that any person was subservient to myself.

Come August, with still a month to go before school began and Vernon also on holiday, he decided that we would drive to Mexico! Oh dear. It would in fact be the first of many visits, and in time we spent much of his retirement years there, but in that hot summer, already full of new impressions and preoccupations, I was ready to sit and draw breath in Arlington. But of course to Mexico we went, and of course as always on our holidays Vernon planned it well, made it interesting and ensured that we all got pleasure from it. Jim, the born tourist and traveller, probably absorbed the most but David, not quite eight years old, readily joined in.

We drove through our first desert and saw cacti growing. We stayed in colonial San Miguel de Allende where a dog stole the butter which I had naively put out to cool. We experienced a small earthquake in Mexico City and a large dose of Montezuma's Revenge in Acapulco. (With experience the boys settled on a safe diet of bacon sandwiches and Fanta, an innocuous orange drink.) For the first of many times we climbed (drove) to the top of the tree line on the slopes of Popacatepetl, whose volcanic and usually snow-tipped peak became a familiar friend and landmark as we travelled the country.

Driving through Mexico, 1963

Then home again, to buckle down to the working aspects of our new world. School: James Madison Elementary was at the top of the hill within walking distance. For Jim the new start meant the usual nervous apprehension, but his way was smoothed with the help of a good teacher, the nice Miss Nice, who wrote at the end of his first year that he had been a pleasure to teach. David fitted in well enough, though both had to make similar adjustments, cf: "In the United States we do not add a 'u' in words like favor and color". After the first year Jim transferred to Williamsburg Junior High School, a bus ride away. A harder road, I think, but he did make friends.

IT'S ODD, THE THINGS ONE REMEMBERS

Vernon drove into D.C. daily in our one car. Buses? – they existed, but none of our neighbours would think of using them, nor indeed knew much about them unless in charitable mood they sometimes drove the maid to the bus stop. So we bought me a car (Bouncer had gone to her grave in Ottawa long before) – a compact Ford Falcon sedan, red, in which I learned to navigate the complex numbered streets of our neighbourhood, the George Washington Parkway, the bridges across the Potomac, the narrow roads of Georgetown and the fearsome traffic circles of the city.

I needed to occupy my time. We were not interested in the expense and obligations of joining a Club, which was where the social life of many of our neighbours centred. Of course I had to be available for any DRB functions that arose, but they would mostly be evening affairs. I went occasionally, with the children, to a Unitarian church in Maryland (I had become a regular member of the Unit. Congregation at home in Ottawa) but didn't find any strong attachment there. I might have enjoyed making a garden, but the poor sandy soil and the heat of the summer months discouraged me. The few plants I introduced languished; opined my father when visiting: "this plot is ungardenable!"

Then one day came a suggestion from my long-time friend and mentor, Margaret Watson; she and Gordon were already on their second tour in Washington and he had been instrumental in ensuring Vernon's posting. Said she, why don't you come to a meeting of the International Womens' Federation? You can look at a list of the different groups to see what might interest you. This I did, and joined a choir (enter another new, lively and loyal friend, Joyce Snarr); a French conversation group and an exercise class. I don't remember how frequently we met, or where – no wonder I learned to drive my way around – but all these gave me great pleasure and made interesting friendships.

Vernon meanwhile was finding his feet rapidly, and well. To be working with Gordon was a great bonus and probably alleviated any new-boy nervousness. In particular his path was eased, as were those of his colleagues, by a most exceptional secretarial staff. For the women (naturally they were all women in those days, and single) as for the men, the standard of acceptance at Defence HQ was high. These young ladies were bright, highly qualified, attractive and discreet. They took their jobs seriously and were determined to make the most of their privileges. Dorothy, Frankie and two or three others became almost as familiar to us wives as to the men they worked for and were included in most of our parties. If Vernon, like the others, was somewhat magnetised by this formidable flower power I could not begrudge, and was secretly amused by it. However, seeing how he admired them raised my competitive spirit somewhat; I vowed that on return to Ottawa I too would "go to work" and show what I could do! A naïve assumption; few men could be expected to make such a comparison between wife and office help – nor understand such a motive – though in fact four years later it was with his encouragement that I did return to part-time secretarial work.

So, life in Washington was everything we had expected, enlivened even beyond its customary dignity by the young and charismatic Kennedy family. We felt fortunate that our posting was at this time, when the eyes of much of the western world were turned so favourably on the occupants of the White House.

Until the twenty-second of November, 1963.

"Where were you when President Kennedy was shot?"

Me, I was driving home from somewhere, down the hill and nearly at my own corner when a news bulletin flashed on the car radio. I pulled over and stopped at the side of the road, wondering if I had heard aright. Drove home in a daze. Soon after David appeared from school, bewildered and somewhat disgruntled: "they said, Mr. Kennedy's been shot, and teacher and all the girls started crying!" Next came Jim, sombre, then Vernon – all offices, all businesses, indeed all of the District of Columbia having shut down.

IT'S ODD, THE THINGS ONE REMEMBERS

For three days we lived by the television set. On the day of the funeral we drove, along with hundreds of others, to Arlington Cemetery. Fortunate to get close to the road we watched the cortege pass, silence all around until the guns began. Feeling privileged indeed to be so unexpectedly at the forefront of such a shaking event. I wrote a full account and sent it to many; no point in reproducing here something which has been so vastly documented by history. But nothing was the same. We would not be able to say later that we had been part of the Kennedy years. As we had hoped we would be.

Everything and everyone went on, of course. We could only guess what difference the new administration would make to relations with Canada; some of the guesses were anxious ones. But individually we settled into our prescribed routines. There were receptions, some of which we hosted and I needed to remember names and who was married to whom – or not. There were parties at our house and others; there were visitors from Ottawa, and from England came first Vernon's Mum and later my parents. We took Lil out in our new speedboat on the Potomac; she didn't like it much. In compensation we went on a tour of the Robert Kennedy home where she was able to shake Ethel's hand and introduce herself as a proud visitor from England. That, Lil did enjoy. We drove my parents to Florida, even though it was summer; the car so laden with six bodies and gear that a tire blew before long. They learned to enjoy fried chicken in a basket and the white sands of the Keys. My father learned, after a request for "The Gents" brought only perplexed looks, that what he needed was The Mens' Rest Room.

Even Theo briefly reappeared in my life. Some business had brought him to Washington from New York and he visited twice, once for a reasonably amiable family supper ("have you ever tried cointreau on icecream?") and once for a short lunch with me. He was trying to recover from the departure of his wife and child – a bizarre story of which I never learned the whole, but it sounded cruel enough. He had fallen heavily for a beautiful South American girl, married her and as he thought fathered her child. After some months she announced that the child was not his, she had married him for convenience, not love, and was now returning plus baby to her home country. He did not elaborate and I was too shocked to ask. We parted affectionately but never met again.

A very different Washington memory is that in my 40th year I miscarried a child – our final attempt to have a much wanted second daughter. Whether a girl or not, its failure was probably for the best at that advanced age. I received excellent care in a short hospital stay and the matter closed, with only fleeting regrets.

Came the summer of 1966 and time to go home. I think Vernon was reluctant to leave the work he was doing; uncertain what his position would be on return to DRB in Ottawa. But from a family aspect, it was time. Jim was 14 and due to begin High School. Both he and David would find themselves very lacking in the French which they would have automatically been learning if in Canada. Moreover we had begun to notice a slightly materialistic attitude developing which so far they had managed to avoid; the perhaps inevitable comparison of our fairly modest lifestyle with those of neighbours and schoolmates. "Why didn't you choose a house with a swimming pool?" – "You really should join a club" – "We have such ordinary cars – you should get a more expensive one". None of it too serious, but it might have become so had they stayed longer in the U.S.A.

Equally important was the need to catch up on Mary's life. As promised she had joined us for holidays twice a year – Vernon making the long round trip to collect and return her, staying overnight at Charlie's Motel in Smiths Falls. However, one well-remembered New Year, having seen her safely in, he turned round and drove south through the night – a 20-hour round trip – because he didn't want to miss a special New Year Party!

So, farewells all round and many promises to keep in touch, especially with the Knox and Please families from the World Bank and our lively next door neighbours the Kendricks. (Which, in all three cases, we did.) Another huge moving van, moving away from 3616

N. 36th Road, and ourselves later following in the aforementioned caravan of two cars-one trailer-one boat. I hoped when we reached the Canadian border that the Customs officers wouldn't be too interested in our menagerie. They did scrutinize carefully the health certificate for Winston the cockatiel but the cat was not disturbed. (Only one cat. We had buried Blackie in the Arlington garden when she died of a mysterious "tropical virus". On her grave we had laid a huge arrangement of flowers with which I had been presented at some reception. It's odd, the things one remembers).

The Caravan - Leaving Washington, July, 1966

CHAPTER 7

OTTAWA AGAIN. GROWING UP AND AWAY

Ottawa, 1970 - With David (l), Vernon, and Jim (r)

We had sold the Erindale Drive house. The street had become a bus route and busy with traffic. As well, with savings from the Washington years we could afford somewhat better. Ottawa was expanding and builders were filling acres of farmland with fairly pleasant suburbs. We chose Graham Park, a few miles west of our previous home, with its own new elementary school and two high schools, also new. However we had to wait six weeks for our house to be finished, so short-leased a small townhouse close by. Two moves in so short a time was a nuisance and especially hard on the boys who, adjusting once again to new schools, needed a settled home. To me however it was all worthwhile because this new house, our tenth home in twenty-one years of marriage, was a delight to me. Well planned and finished, with many attractive details of my own choosing, it was well suited to our casual lifestyle and contemporary furniture. Vernon and I set upon it the peculiar seal of our approval by installing a deep red carpet through the entry hall and up the stairs. A guest at one of our housewarmings observed "that's a real Smith gesture". I could have wondered what she meant, but was too pleased with my new nest to care.

Only the garden was rather without character; standard suburban rectangle of 75'x100' open to the street at front and unadorned lawn behind. We planted a few trees, a row of poplars along the back, a flowerbed under the windows. But many things precluded gardening; my return to part-time work, the boys' increasingly busy lives, Vernon's preoccupation with his own resettlement (which was proving to be hard) – no, the attractions of the Brian Crescent house were strictly internal.

We lived there for nine years. When we arrived Jim at 13 began High School, David at 9 had one more year of elementary. By the time we left Jim, strengthened by a long-overdue confidence in himself, had graduated with honours, survived a year-long trek, hippie-style, to north India and back, and begun university.

Oh, that was a great Odyssey indeed; and needs more telling than I can ever give – much I will never know about. Vernon gave Jim a return airline ticket to Singapore. No money, (until, under tearful insistence from me, he grudgingly produced $100 to "get him started"). It was Vernon's way of encouraging Jim's love of travel but to me it was throwing my child in at the deep end of a pool I did not think him ready to navigate. He was only seventeen! I spent some anguished weeks before his return. Of course he not only survived but was vastly enriched and his experiences influenced his future.

IT'S ODD, THE THINGS ONE REMEMBERS

By the time he was 18 years old, David had developed a serious talent for rock music, opening a new and competitive world for himself. Entirely by his own efforts and with little encouragement from uncomprehending parents, particularly father, he later formed a good band and enjoyed some heady successful years. They made records, toured the breadth of Canada, once briefly topped the charts in Italy – have you not heard of Roman Grey?

But that was to come later. At school's end he in turn received his airline ticket to adventure, in his case found in Australia. I seem to have worried less about him. He had some paying jobs, found new friends, and was not so long away. He returned safely to Canada 10 months later, zooming into our Richmond driveway on a friend's motorbike.

In spite of the pleasant home, good new neighbours and friends, and my personal satisfaction with my new modest role as a wage earner, the years 1966 to 1975 were not easy. As he had half expected, Vernon found his return to DRB Headquarters unsatisfactory. "I opened a drawer in my old desk and there was a calendar I had left there four years ago. Nothing has changed!" As well, his adolescent sons were not as malleable or accepting of his wisdom as his eager small boys had been. There were arguments and clashes of opinion – even, I later realised, a subconscious jealousy now, seeing them as rival males for my attention. He began to drink too much. I dreaded seeing the bottle of rye appear as soon as he came home, and dinner times became tense and miserable instead of a looked-forward to family ritual. Then during this decade both my father and Vernon's mother died, necessitating sad short trips to England for us both. Two much-loved grandparents were lost at a time when we badly needed the strength of family ties.

Withal, we still had some good holidays; we all got on better away from home! and escapes to Blue Sea Lake now included groups of school friends to enjoy the fun of water skiing with the new boat brought from Washington. In fact our house was continually enlivened by the comings and goings of Jim's and David's friends. Apparently Vernon and I were more "open-minded" than some 1970s parents.

Within reason we tolerated long hair, smoking (Vernon was known to share a joint occasionally) and beer (so long as too many cases of empties didn't accumulate under the bed). Overnight refugees were often found in the basement bedroom. Of course most of them turned out just fine and a handful now well into middle age have remained close friends.

We also had some interesting longer-term guests. There was Philippe Perron, son of my cousin Winifred Bentley. Winnie had married a penniless French Baptist minister, had five children and decided that Philippe the eldest should seek his fortune in Canada. Through contacts in Paris she found him a job in a small Revlon outlet in Ottawa, so Philippe lived for some months in our basement while testing shades of lipstick for a small wage and improving his English. He failed to convert any of us to his fundamentalist religious beliefs but greatly enjoyed sharing David's musical ventures, which were by now becoming a serious part of David's life. We introduced Phil to a French Baptist minister in Ottawa for whom he went to work, eventually marrying his younger daughter and taking her back to France.

A more exotic lodger was Bashir Amani. Elder son of a wealthy Afghan politician anxious to get his children out of the country, and whose daughters were already at American universities, Bashir had been sent to Canada and arrived at Carleton University. With Jim now away from home and his room vacant, Vernon and I had responded to requests for accommodation for foreign students and were given an address in the Glebe where two such young men were lodging. As we entered and asked if either were interested in coming to stay with us, this lively dark-eyed one leapt to his feet and said "Yes! I get my things!" Which he very quickly did and in short order we three were in the car on our way to Bashir's new billet.

With Bashir Amani – backyard of the Brian Crescent house, 1972

He was the same age as Jim, but by then Jim had left home. However David bonded well with Bashir and was a help to him with the many adjustments to both academic and social life. A small family in a relatively simple house must have been very different from a sprawling compound of many dwellings and many generations in the heart of Kabul, but Bashir was eager to fit in and he did so well. His English became good and he enjoyed his months with us. He left Canada with a BA in Political Science and some understanding of the ways of the west – major factors in his later survival

Returning to Afghanistan – war-torn, Russian-occupied and bitterly divided – he found his father imprisoned and soon to be executed, a victim of his too-close connections to the king and the ousted ruling party. Bashir was able to get his mother and younger brother safely to a sister in New York. I believe that he himself "went to ground" and had some difficult and dangerous years. He tried, but failed, to return to Canada. Eventually, after hardships and setbacks at which I can only guess, he went with a wife and two children to Germany and has established himself in a thriving business near Dusseldorf. He telephones and emails me regularly with pressing invitations to visit. There are scars, though, on this relatively happy ending. His mother died in her seventies in poor health, and the cherished brother who was still a child during the worst years in Afghanistan lives now in a psychiatric hospital near to Bashir.

I often wonder, but do not ask him, what have been Bashir's thoughts these last ten years as he watched this most recent despoliation of his country, ultimately as fruitless as all such attempts have been by would-be conquerors for centuries past!

Foreign visitor number three was Marianne Schneider from Berlin. She did not stay long enough to qualify as a lodger, but she was an interesting and rather challenging guest for a short time. Vernon had met her in California, he on a business trip, she on vacation "standing in line to get into Disneyland". From a NATO assignment in Germany some months later Vernon returned home earlier than scheduled with only vague explanations; "I wanted to come home". Then began arriving in the mail interesting packages; small presents of penholders, desk accessories, frequent fat letters with lots of stamps. Said Vernon with some embarrassment " they are from this friend who would like to come and visit; would it be all right?" Well of course I could hardly wait! We painted the furniture in the spare bedroom, bought new bedlinen, and I shopped hopefully for the kinds of savoury things which I knew German people preferred for breakfast.

Marianne was trim, dark-haired, animated, very smartly dressed and very bright; her English was perfect. We showed her the sights, took her out on the boat, Vernon drove her to Toronto for the day. She relaxed in the garden while I went off to work; she found our cuisine interesting. I was mostly terrified but of course we got on fine; after she left more interesting packages began to arrive, this time they

IT'S ODD, THE THINGS ONE REMEMBERS

were presents for me! There were phone calls from time to time; we heard of poor health and depression – "I would love to come and visit you in Mexico!" By this time the communication was mainly between Marianne and me – Vernon, exhausted by the complications to his orderly ways, had lost interest! Though of course I was glad that he did not apparently want to pursue, or be pursued any further (in Marianne's words "so, you will not be more than a friend to me!") I was also pleased and amused that he had been tempted. In view of my own folly in 1955 he could never have been faulted had he embarked on an adventure of his own. But he side-stepped it, and I felt luckier than I deserved.

The "Brian Crescent years" contained also my own resumption of my connection with ODAMR, the association which Mrs. Kehoe had launched 25 years before. Now came wider recognition of the needs of the mentally handicapped and both federal and provincial dollars were coming the way of such groups, (expediting amongst other ventures the transfer of people like Mary from hospital schools to integration in the community).

In 1970 I was chairman of the Residential Care Committee of that organisation and so had the huge satisfaction of opening our very first Group Home in the Ottawa area. We leased from the National Capital Commission a lovely heritage property in quiet grounds near Bells Corners. To the original fine old stone house we added two more buildings, developed an agricultural program and made a secure home for fifteen people with very special needs. Other group homes opened in and around the city but Silver Spring Farm remains my special pride. Forty years later I remain close friends with some of the original staff; I still, at the age of 95, volunteer and share in their activities every week.

Now Vernon began seriously to consider an early retirement. He was not alone in his discontent with the changing face of the Defence Research Board . Its role in Canadian Defence policy was diminishing as the latter was increasingly being shaped and influenced by that of

125

the U.S.A. Vernon was increasingly being side-tracked into "management" positions in which he had no interest; his pleasure in his work had always come from its scientific and analytical aspects. However, he most happily discovered that he could "buy back" his period of R.A.F. service to add to his pension. After much paperwork, advice and guidance from the experts he did retire in December 1975 – at the age of fifty-five.

Most eagerly he made plans for this next life stage. Foremost, we must escape Canadian winters. Not ready by age or inclination to sit on a Florida beach, his interest turned increasingly to Mexico which had so attracted us both on our visits there, and which represented a cheaper and more challenging alternative to the southern United States.

Plans, once made, were carried out with speed. No need for a big house? We would find a small place away from Ottawa, live cheaply there for two thirds of the year and even more cheaply in Mexico for the winter months. Jim and David ? They should fend for themselves. Jim had been independent, if precariously, for several years; David at nineteen could do likewise. But oh, my misgivings about leaving them for so long! This for me was the hard part.

CHAPTER 8

RICHMOND AND MEXICO

Mexico – 1970s

On a map we drew a circle of 15km radius around Ottawa. (If Jim and David were to be abandoned we should at least be within shouting distance?). We bought a small bungalow in Richmond, a village we knew and liked. We sold my "dream house" at a good price, and after a six-month interval of downtown apartment living while Vernon tied up loose ends at DRB and I completed an exceptionally satisfying bilingual assignment in a Defence Department branch "across the river", out to the country we went. Jim had moved out of the Brian Crescent home several years previously and was now at Carleton University; David, with his musical future tentatively shaping up, also found shelter with friends, and soon headed off on his own adventure across the world.

We lived in Richmond from 1975 to 1985, but closed the house each November and drove to Mexico, returning in February or March. So for 7-8 months of the year we became good villagers, growing and freezing our vegetables, riding our bicycles, helping at the library and the annual fair. In winter, driving our carefully loaded car we became familiar with different routes south through the States, with the desert highways of northern Mexico, mastering the art of crossing Mexico City on the "periferico", and in time exploring much of that fascinating, varied country.

For the first few years I had mixed feelings about this new venture. I felt very uneasy about leaving the children – they *were* still children! None of my friends' offspring were yet out of the nest. They had little or no money – were they eating? – staying out of danger/trouble/hardship? However, once we were established in our tiny casitas in Tepoztlan or Puerto Escondido both Jim and David were able to visit at different times. Rapture for mother! – and assured me that my fears were needless. "We don't worry about you and Dad, you need not worry about us".

Vernon of course did not worry. He was living his dream. Indeed he planned our travels so well, made the adventure interesting while taking every care for our safety and my comfort, that I would be churlish not to appreciate, relax and enjoy. In fact after a time I became the more Mexican-ised of the two of us. We both took Spanish lessons but I used it more and became fluent. I shopped, cooked, met the neighbours and the market ladies, trained my 15 year-old muchacha in the way I wanted the floors mopped and the sheets hung out – and I *walked*. How I enjoyed exploring on foot in all the places we stayed. I learned the lanes and hidden corners of dusty villages, the pine-shaded paths up the lower slopes of Popocatapetl, and the long beaches, the donkey tracks and the questionably-smelling alleys of our "holiday home", Puerto Escondido. I never felt unsafe. We had had the sense to learn the basics of travel far from home; dress plainly, wear no jewellery,

IT'S ODD, THE THINGS ONE REMEMBERS

learn the language, stay in after dark. And stay where the people are; there were always people everywhere so just be among them.

We divided our time between two very different but equally attractive places; first heading south from Mexico City, away from its smog and over the surrounding plateau, about 100km. to the old town of Tepoztlan. Its cobbled streets straggled down the hillside from the central plaza, lively like all Mexican communities with people, animals, chickens, music, and flowers. The native population was enlarged at weekends and holidays by city dwellers who maintained properties there, who were only too pleased to have their "casitas" or gatehouses occupied in their absence by presumably reliable visitors. Thus we lived extremely cheaply for two months or more in one such fully equipped cottage while enjoying the owners' pool, garden and the bounty of their orchard: kumquats, bananas, peaches we gathered there. Jim, Jacquie and David were able to join us briefly and at different times.

We made many friends; Mexican and German, American and Canadian, a few in Tepoztlan but more in the larger more cosmopolitan and historic Cuernavaca, a short drive "down the highway" to the plains below. We went there frequently, not only to enjoy slightly warmer temperatures than our cool mountainside, but to stock up at one of the new supermarkets – oh, taste of home! – Despite the charms and surprises of the Tepoztlan " mercado" and the tiny shops, it was sometimes useful to find familiar items such as Tetley's Tea and Kellogg's Corn Flakes and good quality household items. Thirty years on I still possess a sturdy bath towel almost unmarked by time.

After Christmas – and Christmas in Mexico is a fiesta indeed! – it was on to our "seaside holiday". Packing up and driving again, on more adventurous and varied routes than the speedy smooth North American thruways, south to the Pacific coast and the town of Puerto Escondido, the "hidden port" some distance to the southeast of Acapulco.

Originally it would have been like scores of others up and down the same coast; small, poor, scrubby, and sparsely populated with fishing the main source of any income. But around the 1960s young and adventurous foreigners, also for the most part scrubby and poor themselves, began to explore and find haven in these remote spots, bringing their music, their drugs and unfettered lifestyle with them. Our own first knowledge of Puerto Escondido's existence came in the form of a postcard from Jim Smith! – discovering this remote part of the Mexico coast in the course of his adventurous early travels.

After the "hippies" came the surf boarders as word spread of the two perfect sandy bays; they come still, and a string of their original thatched cabins lines "the surfing beach" to this day. Inevitably the town grew, attracted more affluent visitors, built hotels and guest houses, and developed a loyal group of returning long and short term visitors, ourselves and our family among them. A very special such return was on the occasion of my 90th birthday when David and Heidi, Jim and Jacquie and I were able to spend a few days there all together; indeed David and Heidi now return as often as they can, expanding their knowledge of and affection for "P.E." and the surrounding area.

However in Vernon's and my first visits this development was in very early stages. We stayed on the beach in a small complex of casitas which were built and managed by the enterprising local dentist and his efficient senorita. Spare, small but efficient, the little houses gave escape from the heat of the day and the variety of their inhabitants guaranteed lively company. As in Tepoztlan we soon evolved the pleasant routine of market, cafes, open-air laundering and long afternoon siestas, here with the added joys of ocean swims and greeting the fishing boats as they brought in the morning catch.

IT'S ODD, THE THINGS ONE REMEMBERS

Top: on the front porch with my friends the hippies and surfers, Puerto Escondido.
Below: Puerto Escondido, the back of our house is in the foreground, centre.

Tepotzlan – and the distinctive mountain bowl in which it sits; Upper right, the local buses on which explored much of the central plateau; Below, our casita.

IT'S ODD, THE THINGS ONE REMEMBERS

We did not idle away all our time in Mexico on flowery terraces and sunny beaches. From both our "bases" we went exploring. Thanks to Vernon's excellent and untiring driving; to a succession over the years of (mostly) reliable Ford sedans and with our own increasing confidence in language and knowledge of the ways and wiles of the country, we covered much ground.

From Tepoztlan we drove to Puebla and on eastward to "el Rico Cuidad de Veracruz" – the Rich City of the Golden Cross. (But chiefly it is a large port redolent of fish and engine oil). Then on to the Yucatan peninsula, the ruins of Tulum and Chichen Itza; motels and inns, varying in size and efficiency but all cheap, and with sensible precautions always we felt safe.

From Puerto Escondido we headed up through scrubby hills to Oaxaca – another Mexico, another culture; becoming more pronounced when one year we struck south again to St. Cristobal de las Casas – pausing of course on the way at the ancient site of Palenque. Such sombre temples, pressed into the deep sides of the jungly cliffs! Having gone so far, why not across the border into Guatemala? Of course. A poorer, uneasier echo of Mexico , more guarded in approach to visitors, but colourful and fascinating still. Driving was more adventurous; armed guards were stationed at many bends in the road, but their purpose was not very evident.

At a high look-out above Guatemala City an American looked at our car licence plate in disbelief: "Say, can I take a picture?". Then he smiled and said, "Well I guess you just came a long way."

Yes, we did.

Sadly by about 1980 Vernon's back and legs were becoming increasingly stiff; a history of slipped discs and two operations over the previous decade was catching up with him. Fortunately he was comfortable with the long distance driving, but walking was painful. He peacefully installed himself in garden or on beach, with "cerveza" or rum and coke at hand; often friends for company and a dip in the pool or the sea.

An idyll indeed; but the months in Richmond were more complex. For the first few years I continued the part-time contract work with the federal government which I had been doing with increasing confidence and satisfaction since 1970. But Vernon's vision of retirement had not included the absence of a wife for seven hours of the day, the need to make his own breakfast and lunch and – worse – the expectation that he might begin preparations for an evening meal. He became at times quite truculent and bad-tempered. Eventually it became pointless to continue – too wearing, too distracting – and I gave up, handing in my notice at a particularly interesting job with (then) Indian Affairs and Northern Development, much to my boss's bewilderment and my own disappointment.

Relieved of some, though not all of that stress, I quite enjoyed "fulltime" in the small house and big garden, cycling everywhere on the dead-flat roads around the neighbourhood, helping in the library, entertaining my city and suburban friends by proudly serving them the results of my new talents with preserves, sauces and salads from our home grown herbs and vegetables. For a while I was, as in childhood, a village girl again.

Then came two important family happenings; a gain and a loss:

While Vernon and I were shaping our retirement life, Jim's time was hardworking and busy. About two years after graduating from Carleton University, and working at various jobs in Ontario, he obtained a grant to the London School of Economics and graduated well with his MSc. – a hard-won accomplishment of which to be proud. He then held a number of positions with different employers, one of which was with the National Planning Office in Papua New Guinea who hired him to help develop economic policies for the newly-independent country. A long way from home indeed; but any uncertainties there were in such strange surroundings were offset by a meeting which profoundly affected his life and by extension the rest of our family's.

In Port Moresby at that time there was also a young Australian teacher of English working in the Ministry of Education, helping them develop course material. And so Jacqueline Rust came into our lives. She married Jim, gave us three most exceptional grandchildren and broadened our horizons to include her Melbourne family who we came to know and cherish. For the next 25 years Jacquie's many skills, her steadfast commitment to the job in hand and adaptation to whatever came her way, made secure and happy homes with Jim and their children (in seven countries on four continents!), travelling and adapting constantly and making global citizens of them all.

Jim and Jacquie - Papua New Guinea, 1980

From Papua New Guinea, Jim worked briefly in Indonesia for a British consulting firm and then obtained a position with the World Bank – remember friend David Knox in Arlington? – Again, something to be proud of. Jim shaped a fine and satisfying career for himself, and his early retirement from "the Bank" has left him with a network of good friends and colleagues around the world with whom he and

Jaquie keep in touch. As well, some of the similarities between their peripatetic lives and those of my brother and Pat have made for some interesting mutual recollections and a very enriching family bond.

That was the *gain* of the 1980s. The loss was the death of my mother. Not so much her dying; at 86 she had a stroke and deteriorated slowly in mind and body – but the fact that she died while I was in Mexico and totally unable to get to England. By a cruel coincidence Vernon was at the same time isolated in our Tepoztlan cottage with a severe case of Hepatitis B. I could neither leave him nor ask anyone to stay with him. It was a bitterly sad week or two, with only a few difficult long distance phone calls, my blessed brother ever comforting and trying to reassure: "there is nothing you can do". Nothing maybe – except to be there with Mama and with him, when I should have been.

Vernon recovered, we packed up and headed home. On the day of my mother's burial beside my father in Sutton Valence churchyard (beside that same path whose way he had cleared of brambles for me on my wedding day) we were driving through Cincinnati. As we crossed the wide river on a long high-arched iron bridge Vernon, driving, gently put his hand on my knee.

Later that year I went to help Bill empty the little house, Candle Way, where she had spent 17 years as a widow. For the first few days there I was alone, which I cherished. Taking things to the Thrift Store – her hats in which she looked so charming, were dismissed with a "thank you – please leave them on that shelf" … trying to decide between the garbage bin and the yes-we-will-keep-them-awhile. Bill came with a van and carried all the latter home to store in his barn. For years to come on visits to England I would creep into that barn and turn over the boxes, the damp papers, rub dust off the yellow and black tea set which had been "very best" for all our childhood; try to decide how much mattered – or not. In time it all became less important; has moulded or disappeared, and I, now older by two years than Mama was when she died, understand how exactly the same ritual will be repeated by my children when my lares and penates must be disposed

IT'S ODD, THE THINGS ONE REMEMBERS

of. It matters so little – so very, very little. Of far greater meaning and abiding strength to me is her presence, and it is continually with me. I hear her advice; I ask her questions and receive the answers; I am astonished and humbled to find how constant is my mother's influence and guidance, as strong now as ever it was. What a testimony to that complex, conflicted, but beloved person; truly she is "woven into the fabric of my being". I shall *never* be without her.

Back in Richmond we planted a maple sapling for her in the front garden. But it did not survive, and by then we had decided to sell the bungalow and move back to Ottawa.

CHAPTER 9

HOME TO ROOST

By the start of 1985, Vernon's deteriorating physical health was limiting his activities and frustrating him. Pain and stiffness in legs and back now took all pleasure from gardening, painting or repairs; he wanted to reserve his strength for the travel which meant so much to him. Diagnoses were inconclusive; initially a tentative one was made for Multiple Sclerosis. "I am 99.5% sure you have MS" said a cautious doctor. Although eventually proved wrong, this was sufficient to begin the search for more maintenance-free living.

In fact we didn't need to search for long. Choosing to return to the western edge of Ottawa which we knew so well, we found a new 6 storey condominium building overlooking Britannia, the park, the village and the bay. Our roomy north-facing apartment there, with its splendid view of the river and the Gatineau hills, its fitted carpets, a Jacuzzi bathtub and big windows, seemed quite posh after the little country bungalow. In spite of some regret at leaving my garden I settled quite readily, and more than thirty years later I am contentedly still there – three times longer that I have lived anywhere else.

Mexico of course must not be abandoned. Vernon still felt comfortable driving and we planned a "positively last" visit for early 1986 with a very special stopover in Washington to meet Jacquie and Jim's first baby, our wonderful granddaughter Jessica Ann. A short, happy, confused visit, parents tired but jubilant, baby tucked into a dresser drawer, new grandmother kneeling at the bath tub washing a mountain of tiny clothes and trying to find places to dry them. I left reluctantly, anxious for the new parents' well-being (I don't seem to have been at all anxious about that rosy baby) – but relieved to know that Jacquie's parents would be arriving soon from Australia. A little over two months later we had the joy of welcoming them all to Tepoztlan and meeting Cecily and Bernhard for the first time, showing them our home from home, sharing mutual delight in Jessie; ("she has only grown a little bit in 6 weeks" says my diary. "More round, more golden haired, more good-looking; her aunt Fiona in faraway Australia, when told that Jessie was perfect, said simply 'of course!').

First Grandchild – Mary (left) and Jacquie, with Jessie, on the front steps of Jim and Jacquie's Washington apartment, 1986.

As an aside here, I am interested to see from diary entries how frequently in the early years of their marriage I thought that Jacquie and Jim might go to live in Australia. Jim knew and liked the country; he had after all no roots in Canada and had already by age 34 spent much time away from here. But they didn't. After another twenty years of varied and colourful – if often challenging– assignments in Indonesia, Nepal and Malawi, punctuated by spells in Washington where Jessie's brothers were born in due course, they came in fact to live in Ottawa, to support us, Mary and me, as they do to this day. Few families would make such a difficult adjustment; few dependent parents and siblings could expect such a commitment. My love and gratitude to Jacquie and Jim is inexpressible.

Adjusting to apartment life was smoother than I expected – maybe I was more ready for it than I had admitted. There was a new garden to be developed and not too many residents interested in doing so, plus the challenge of creating a "balcony garden" with a windy north facing aspect. I served a term on the board of directors – a less professional body in those early days than now, when condominiums have spread like mushrooms and the management of them has become more tightly regulated.

I also began making weekly visits to one of the OCAPDD group homes where some of Mary's friends live, to help with supper and the evening's activities. The Ahearn House is a short walk down the hill towards the river and I have been going there now for over 25 years. In bad weather taking the car, or missing a week due to other commitments, but always bearing "dessert" and receiving enthusiastic welcomes. Thus I became an official volunteer with the Association which I helped to launch more than 50 years ago, spending time with other groups and programs as well. It gives me challenges, firm friendships and enormous satisfaction.

By 1990 Vernon's declining mobility was our main preoccupation and we made a "positively last" drive to Mexico. The farewells to Tepoztlan and to Puerto Escondido were made slightly easier because some of our friends were likewise spending time there no longer – or dying. One winter we flew with a tour group to the state of Narayit on the west coast of Mexico – new ground for us and a new way of seeing it. But car travel was still the most comfortable for Vernon, so with him as excellent navigator I drove us south myself. One year to a retirement complex in Texas on the banks of the Rio Grande, near the Mexican border at Brownsville. So – we parked the car there at the end of the bridge and I pushed the wheelchair and Vernon across! – for one last cerveza in a café on the dusty main street of Matamoros. The next year it was Orlando, Florida – an easy journey and a pleasant enough stay, made even better by visits from Jim, from my cousin Paul White whose own winter refuge was at Cape Canaveral, and from Peggy and Lee Kendrick who had been our lively next-door neighbours in Arlington.

Because of this – "our main preoccupation" – during the 1980s I neglected my children, but of course they survived very well without me. Indeed they achieved goals of which in their very different ways (and how very different are my three children!) they could be proud. David brought his group, Roman Grey, to its best successes, touring Canada and releasing his major album "Edge of the Shadow". At the end of 1988 Jacquie and Jim welcomed David, Jessie's new brother, and I can tell anyone who will listen that it is a very special experience indeed to hold your first grandson in your arms.

Mary still was benefitting from the varieties of Group Homes then available , and by the end of the decade was living in a most satisfactory one, with mates and staff who were to remain constants for her over many changes to come.

David recording the second Roman Grey album, 1985

IT'S ODD, THE THINGS ONE REMEMBERS

The best way to record the rest of 1990 is to quote the letter I sent to family and friends that Christmas:

"Vernon had two spinal operations in August and October in an attempt to alleviate the rapidly deteriorating use of his legs, arms and hands. He was not promised a cure, but at best a halt to the troubles. The first operation in the lower back (lumbar) area did not help, although he recovered well from the actual surgery. So he agreed to a second operation at the base of the neck (3rd vertebra), again quite aware that it might at least give some stabilisation. This operation was done on 29th October.

The actual surgery went as planned but at some stage he sustained damage to his spinal cord. Possibly due to a brief drop in blood pressure but no definite cause has been identified. As a result he lost all movement below the neck, and although he has regained fairly good use of his left hand and movement of his left leg, his right limbs are inert and as yet he can't sit up. Above the neck, praises be, he is perfectly all right - brain, eyes, ears and speech are undamaged.

The prognosis is cautious and contradictory; he may regain enough movement to be able to look after himself; one or two of the attendant doctors say he may walk, but that is hard to imagine at present. He is being well cared for in the most modern of Ottawa's several good hospitals and when strong enough – we hope in December – he will be moved to the excellent Rehabilitation Centre where he will, as he says, be made to work hard. We expect at least six months there; I think myself that many more months of perseverance lie ahead.

All a horrid shock and sorrow to us, and so bitterly ironic that the op. which was his last resort should instead have put him flat on his back. He is philosophical and does not regret the operation; nor can we specifically fault the surgeon since we may never know what happened. Certainly it was a very shaken surgical team who heard him say as he came round from the anaesthetic "Hey! I can't move". And who came to find me, sitting far longer than I had expected to in a drab and bare waiting room, to haltingly describe these results to me.

I am spending every day at the hospital; have great support from wonderful friends and of course from the children. David and Judy spent last weekend with me, visiting Vernon with that mixture of concern and nervous discomfort felt by all who are unfamiliar with hospitals. Jim most valiantly plans to come next weekend, even though he is only just home from five weeks in Asia and expects his third baby in less than a month. Mary keeps me company and prays hard for her Dad.

So, I am quite busy. But I send love and Christmas greetings as always. I know you will all think of us, and that helps no end."

So, overnight our lives changed most drastically. For Vernon indeed it was more of a half-life for the first dreary weeks – stiff, uncomfortable, basically paralyzed from the waist down and enmeshed in the web of hospital routine; he, erstwhile so fiercely independent, now at the mercy of a procession of nurses, doctors, therapists with their intrusions, their pills and their paraphernalia. Yet he was surprisingly enduring and cooperative, usually cheerful with the nurses and always with a smile to greet me. For my part I was forced to create a survival routine of daily visits (a 40-minute round trip if weather and traffic favoured), dealing at home with streams of telephone calls, kindly-meaning visitors, anxious family and official correspondence. My diary of the ensuing weeks, months, is very detailed, perhaps an outlet for my tumbling emotions.

At the end of 2 weeks Vernon was moved to the Rehabilitation Centre where (diary again) "they make all things new. Where all is upbeat and active; people in wheelchairs buzzing around, careful earnest young ladies manoeuvering Vernon's poor floppy body into a totally inadequate chair… in a ward with three other men. Both of us tired, confused and sad". But there did come one very bright ray to brighten us; Jacquie herself phoned me to tell of the arrival of Michael Timothy James, the new brother for Jessie and David . Vernon rejoiced – a wide smile, and "oh I am so glad" he said.

Slowly, with ups and downs, slight improvements followed by frustrating setbacks, we settled in to our new life. Jim and David visited when they could – friends also, in moderation. Mary, bewildered but practical, had good questions: "do you have to brush his teeth? How can he pee and that?" The outside world mostly washed over us, but in January 1991 the American attacks on Baghdad and the start of their war against Iraq made us wonder what more horror we might be facing. However by March I wrote, not altogether flippantly:

"The Gulf War is over.
Spring is coming
Jim will be home soon.
Brother Bill has been to stay."

Vernon has discarded his catheter – and that my friends I vow is every bit as important to us as the ending of the war. I have been to Washington and spent 5 days with Jacquie and the children and met Michael, the last of the three fine-made, healthy, good-looking bright babies.

Vernon began making weekend visits home, and small progresses, though the physical effort for both of us was great. I began to realise that all this was going to go on for a very long time – that both he and I faced a future permanently at home. Well, we agreed in our more cheerful moments, we have done lots of interesting things with our lives, and after all plenty of people our age are in like situations ….

Just don't let it go on too long

The 6 month rehabilitation period was to end in early June, so, encouraged by Vernon I went to England for 10 days – a "last-chance" holiday he called it. Indeed it was memorable, because as well as the blessed balm of Pat and Bill's care in Cumbria, it included a 4-day stay in Coventry for the first Commonwealth Air Forces Radar Reunion. There I reunited with my three best mates from those far-off WAAF years; a most wonderful meeting full of laughter and tears and incredulity that this could really happen. I attended further reunions in later years but none could match that first gathering of people – Canadians, British, Aussies and New Zealanders – sharing 50 year old memories; speaking the same "language". I took with me Vernon's photo albums of his RAF years in the Middle East but wasn't able to find anyone who had been on the same stations.

As for my dear trio, Pauline did come to an Ottawa reunion a few years later, and I visited Daphne at her home in Kent, but within about 12 years all three of them, even the youngest "Jeannie" – who we had sheltered so carefully from 19-year-old pitfalls! – all three of them were dead.

IT'S ODD, THE THINGS ONE REMEMBERS

Radar Reunion – Coventry, 1991; With Daphne (left) and Pauline (right)

On 12th June 1991 Vernon came home. The first day of the rest of our lives.

The elves in Santa's Workshop at the Rehab. Centre had adapted a light wheelchair for him; controls on the left side and a removable electric motor which could be left behind when the chair was folded and put in the car trunk. This was a godsend, because it gave him independence of movement within the apartment and we could – and did – go anywhere we wanted in the car.

As well as the wheelchair there was of course much more necessary equipment. I grew to admire and appreciate the scope of Community and Social Services, an organisation which made our lives so much easier than I had expected. They sent a cheerful handyman to make the bathroom accessible; gave guidance on the purchase of supplies, and most essential of all, set up a roster of home helps to come two or three times a week. For the next eight years this cheerful procession of women and men made our difficult, circumscribed life bearable. Several of them were regulars and became trusted friends, giving me precious away time and to Vernon a change of company. From the earliest days of his trauma he had been unfailingly appreciative of the people – so many people – who ministered to him; he developed a stoicism and patient acceptance of his lot quite at odds with his previous somewhat recalcitrant nature. Though frustrated, tired and uncomfortable, beset by hindrances and with his horizons so cruelly shrunken, yet over those years he became a gentler person. The rocky road on which we now set out was smoother because of this.

Slowly we became more adept at our daily round; resigned to taking much time over small things; Vernon able to slightly use the inert right hand and even walk a few steps. Family came from all quarters, bringing needed cheer; even Cecily and Bernhard from Australia; I remember a complete-family Father's Day picnic in the park. David was a true and practical blessing, staying to put up handrails and shelves and give Vernon his time and his company – the most needed of gifts. Jim had already made three long journeys from far away, one with young David in tow so that Jacquie and Jessie could concentrate on new Michael.

Moreover that peripatetic family was getting ready for a major new move. After much consideration Jim took the offered post of Deputy Mission Head of the World Bank, based in Kathmandu – a three year stint. Two days before they left, Vernon, Mary, the wheelchair, and I spent a few hours with them at Sharbot Lake. A needed spell of quiet (3-children-type quiet) looking out at a Canadian lake, after tiring days of packing up and farewells in Washington.

What a long way away they are going. We won't be able to visit them there.

Maybe not, but we did continue to travel by car; Vernon an expert navigator and I accustomed to long distance driving. At the end of 1991 we spent a few weeks in Ormond Beach, Florida. On the road there were of course a new set of challenges to be met; not all restaurants and washrooms were wheelchair accessible – in any case, was I going to be welcome as an attendant in a Men's? (We were rather proud of the way we solved this one. Park in a secluded spot as near the washrooms as possible, use the plastic pee bottle in the car and Ann takes it in to the Women's for emptying and washing.)

Two more similar excursions in '93 and '94, to Myrtle Beach, Florida and to a small town called Donna in Texas, close to the Mexican border. It was from here that we drove to Brownsville and, as described earlier, I wheeled Vernon across the bridge to Matamoros so he could once again have a cerveza in a Mexican bar. But the journeys became increasingly tiring; uncomfortable for Vernon to sit for long periods, exhausting for me to handle all the packing and unpacking, pit stops, loading and unloading the wheelchair time after time after time, as well as driving. We settled for shorter, less ambitious excursions from home.

Of which the longest and most exciting was in May 1992 to Toronto for David and Judy's wedding. A happy occasion made even more so because the Kathmandu family came, also Pat and Bill from England. Once Vernon was settled in his pew in the church the hateful wheelchair was whisked out of sight by the Two Best Men, Ross R. and Jeff S. ("I couldn't choose between them so I had them both" said David). And Vernon stood up straight for Judy as she came down the aisle. A poignant moment, never forgotten. I didn't know he was going to do it, but had the sense not to put out a helping hand.

It was also in 1992 that I learned of Theo's death, as recounted in Chapter 3. My last letter to him was returned marked 'Deceased' on February 11 – the anniversary of John David's death, and thus did I remember the date.

I mourned this loss deeply. Worse, I was guilt-ridden by the memory of a telephone call I had from him at just the time of Vernon's operation, when I was too distracted to give it the attention he so clearly needed. He spoke of being "at sea" – of wanting to move but he didn't know where to go. "Maybe back to my cabin in the Carolina woods ... anyway, I wanted to talk to someone and I thought, who else but Ann?".

If the postmistress was right in her estimate of his death it must have been very soon after that call. I could not help wondering if he took his own life. I shall never know, and so much not-knowing added hugely to my frustration and distress. All kept to myself of course – I sent an official death notice to the Old Suttonians section of the Sutton Valence School magazine but didn't hear from any of his contemporaries. Flaying myself with more guilt I remembered how in recent years he had urged me to "come and visit the old artist in his eyrie – it isn't so far" and indeed I could have driven across the Eastern Townships to the small Hudson Valley town. But I didn't.

A year or two later Vernon asked after him (we were hanging some of Theo's water colours in the spare bedroom over my newly-installed computer table). When I said that he had died V's response "Oh – I am so sorry to hear that" sounded quite genuine – as I have said he was becoming a mellower person in the face of his own trials.

CHAPTER 10

THE CHALLENGING YEARS

With our own home lives now restricted, family occasions and milestones became more significant – good excuses for celebrations if they were happy ones; marked by extra care if they were not. I have spoken of Judy and David's wedding. In 1994 we had a gathering for my 70th birthday, and Vernon's 74th, which included not only all the family but from England, in addition to Pat and Bill, came Mary Vinson, my friend from infancy whose home, according to the second sentence of this story "is one mile from my house". Also Marion and Tommy McLeod, Jim's godparents and our cherished friends and mentors from earliest Enfield days. Together with many local friends they made a happy group photograph taken on the back patio of Westmount Place. Happy then; bittersweet for me, the survivor, to look at now, because from the eleven there of my own generation only four of us remain ten years later!

Towards the end of 1995, under the heading "… and extra care if they were not" above, came the end of Judy and David's marriage. The causes were not my business to analyse; they had made a pleasant small home in north-east Toronto and Vernon and I had visited them there. We could only provide sympathetic ears when asked; an exchange of letters with Judy's parents who were as unhappy as ourselves; it was hard to be so helpless in the face of David's anguish. Compounded without doubt by the recent breakup of Roman Grey – a breakup he had not thought necessary. It is a testament to his strength of character that he came through all this entirely on his own and without mental or psychological damage, and, most thankfully, found lasting happiness and a strong marriage when Heidi came into his life some years later.

In October 1995 Vernon and I celebrated our 50th wedding anniversary with much contentment and the purchase of the "engagement" ring I had always wanted but never been able to afford, following the theft two years after our marriage of the tiny stones with which we had begun. Finally I had my half-hoop of three diamonds and two sapphires, all stones chosen by ourselves at Goldform Jewellers and made by them with care and empathy. Not many customers, I guess, appear in their 70s and a wheelchair seeking an engagement ring! But what touched me so much about this, and the reason I write of it in detail, is the great and genuine pleasure which Vernon derived from the whole business. He took careful time over the choice of stones – they had to be brought from New York for some reason – and was really happy when with ceremony he finally gave me the finished treasure.

"The sapphires are you and Vernon and the diamonds are the three of us," David opined some time later. "Where is John David" I asked, and immediately he replied that John David was the ring itself, binding us all together.

IT'S ODD, THE THINGS ONE REMEMBERS

50th Anniversary, 1995

1996 brought some good happenings. My brother Bill was awarded the Order of the British Empire for his work connected with the prison system – I should say, "with Her Majesty's Prisons." This was something he took on after his retirement from Shell International (where, not incidentally, Bill had established a respected career and travelled the world). It was a "voluntary" effort which ended up involving several years of hard work and onerous travel all over Britain and to the United States of America and Canada as well. He was mightily and rightly pleased, and we were all very proud. Since at the end of his Shell career he had been a member of the Board of Directors, we have both many times wished our parents could have known of his success. Known what became of that nervous young Oxford graduate who disappeared to Borneo on his first job with the company, all those many years ago.

Bill Bentley; my beloved and precious and only baby brother who is still my strength and stay, who still operates on my wavelength as I on his. How blessed we are that we are still sharing our Very Old Age and are able to be together from time to time. Truly I could not do without you.

My brother Bill Bentley, my strength and stay through the years – At Heathrow airport, 1970s; with Pat at their farm in Cumbria.

IT'S ODD, THE THINGS ONE REMEMBERS

Still in 1996 and still Bentley-connected, I went to Ireland for the first and only time for nephew Justin's wedding to his – now our – Irish Mary. Fleeting visit; driving from Cumbria across North Wales to Anglesey, the ferry, Dublin; now *there's* a handsome city. All Bentley family were gathered together, thanks yet again to Bill's generosity and faultless planning – and on the return ferry ride what should appear but champagne and plastic glasses with the announcement by one Perry Westbrook that he and my young niece Anthea were now officially engaged. Gets infectious ….

That year ended with all my own family here in Ottawa for Christmas. These visits entailed so much long travel for the Js, and David's time off work was always hard-won, and while here they all did so very much to help Vernon and me, I never have ceased to appreciate the efforts they made over those difficult years. But we made sure there were fun times as well. Snowballs and toboggans; a novelty for the grandchildren who were currently living in Malawi!

Coming now to the year 1997 when Vernon's life, and by extension my own, became more difficult, more tiring and more uncertain. Through February and March there were hospital stays to monitor erratic heartbeats, breath shortage, problems with waterworks – from which he came home exhausted and depressed. "I feel I have changed somehow". True. Up until now he had been thankfully so mentally well but now, though still not losing his marbles so much as simply losing interest.

The 24 hour care routine became increasingly tiring, for Vernon no less than for me and his helpers. As he became weaker there was more need for moving and lifting, occasional falls – on one memorable occasion, when no strong neighbour was available, I had to call the Fire Department as I had been told I was entitled to do. Within minutes a full size fire truck arrived; three very full size firemen in large boots charged cheerfully into the bedroom, lifting Vernon from the floor as if he were a feather. Settling him safely in his chair, with a friendly wave they were off again – "not at all ma'am – it's a pleasure!"

There were even two brief periods when we had to bring oxygen cylinders in. How frightening it was to hang the grim warning signs on the apartment door.

And how fortunate we were with those people, provided through Community Care Services, who came almost every day, for a few hours morning or evening, sometimes both. We were lucky to keep two or three regulars who became trusted companions. There was Cathy Vermette, married to David who made me a banana stand and then inconsiderately died. But left Cathy with us, dependable and loyal, patient and greatly depended on by me in particular because she was able to stay in daytime hours so that I could do needed shopping and appointments. Later I learned that Cathy had received an award for her work with Community Care; I cheered at that.

There was – is – of course, Yvonne. Yvonne who came to Canada with a young daughter – other offspring left behind in Jamaica and the USA. Yvonne who, seeking stability, married Derek and became Yvonne Walker. She sought Vernon's advice on that and many other matters, and battled many a personal demon while unfailingly giving us the special support we increasingly needed. Yvonne from whom Vernon apparently extracted a promise that she would "look after Ann". Yvonne who now as I write 20 years later is a very happy Yvonne Francis, remains a constant loyal friend who because of that promise telephones me every week and says that she will be here for me when I need her. How many people can claim that kind of commitment? More about Yvonne later.

But even the "spares" were always competent and reassuring. I was relieved and touched by Vernon's acceptance of this constant procession of outsiders into the practical side of his daily life – a side which now, sadly, occupied more and more time. But as I said earlier, he was showing a new grace and forbearance quite at odds with his innate impatience.

Throughout, the best supports were of course Jim and David; whenever they could be, they were here, when they could not, they telephoned and Vernon was strengthened and cheered by their calls.

This up and down pattern of our days continued through 1998. The computer and television set (especially watching recordings of his favourite operas) were useful companions. We occasionally went out in the car, but visits to restaurants, stores or the homes of friends involved tiring ins-and-outs from car to wheelchair and back, and Vernon had lost interest in just "driving around to look at the scenery". Visits *from* friends however gave him much pleasure. At the top of the list of loyal and faithful callers was dear Otto Fisher who came every week unfailingly for the last two years of Vernon's life, even to the confusing final days; Otto in fact was his last visitor. Jim Irvine also began to call on us weekly, and another ex DRB colleague and friend, Graham Thistle, slithered on icy roads from Manotick some winter days.

In September things were going smoothly enough that I was encouraged to "take a break" so with only some trepidation I did go once again to England. For eight memorable days my tireless Bill drove us from London to Cumbria, to Worcestershire and Yorkshire and points between. I saw many Smiths and Bentleys and branches thereof (including the newest great-nephew Jack who arrived half way through my visit); I walked again through Sutton Valence and, seated in the churchyard by our parents' gravestone, told them all my adventures.

Yet I was anxious to get home. Had I been selfish to leave Vernon so long – how could I ever have considered doing so? I was met at the airport by kind neighbour John Doyle and my memory of our return to the flat is so vivid that it remains one of my best. There was Vernon wheeling his chair to meet me; smiling brightly, groomed and trim in his ironed yellow shirt, helper Cathy in the background – "we have managed just fine but I'm very glad to see you".

All was well!

And remained more or less so for some weeks. But at the end of November Vernon began intermittent periods of bad coughing and once again the cumbersome oxygen cylinders had to be brought in. On December 1st the overnight caregiver took one look at him on her arrival and said that if we didn't get him to hospital "he's not going to last the night". Looking back – oh how easy it is to look back! – I could have said that we would let him be; not subject him to more upheaval and confusion; that I would take the chance, for both of us; only leave him in peace. But I had come to rely on the opinions of the professionals – they had served us well so far – so off to hospital in the ambulance we went, and Vernon with an oxygen mask lay in a bed and I sat in a comfortable chair. Occasionally we talked: "Are you comfortable enough there?" he asked me once. He had by now pneumonia and acute lung congestion. A long, strange, dreamy sort of night it was. As he slept I found the duty doctor and with the courage of desperation (a cliché, but that *is exactly* what it was) I told her that Vernon had a signed Living Will and would she if necessary honour it? To my huge relief and satisfaction she said yes, there would be no problem with that. Next morning after I had gone home for a few hours' sleep I returned to find him moved to a ward, awake and alert – he had bounced back yet again! But the same doctor was beside him and gently spoke: "Mr. Smith, you know that you are dying. Do you want to stay here with us and we will make you comfortable or do you want to go home?" There could only be one answer to that and he gave it clearly.

Home we came.

Still I did not alarm Jim or David; still we moved through our careful days, the coughing sporadic but manageable. When people asked I told them, yes he is weaker, and talking is becoming more difficult, but Vernon is here.

Came the evening of December 7th when, with a new but very empathetic and physically strong caregiver on hand, I took a leisurely bath before relieving him – "yes thank you John I can manage now; we will be fine" – and settling myself and Vernon for the night. He was

IT'S ODD, THE THINGS ONE REMEMBERS

by now coughing incessantly and couldn't speak; it was distressing but I stroked his chest and tried to calm him and held his hands. Let's be quiet now I said. Let's be peaceful and rest together; we will go to sleep. Quiet the struggle, I said; there is just you and me here now.

Suddenly and completely the dreadful coughing stopped – all at once – completely. Thank heaven he is asleep, I thought. Then he gave two small twitches and was still, and I knew that he was dead.

So we did indeed rest together, all night long, and I held his hands as they slowly grew cooler. What else would I have done? I knew that when morning came I would have to let the world in but these hours still belonged to us; I did not want them to end. I did get up to take a photograph of him; it is a fine one, quite noble looking – I even found a rose to lay on the pillow – which would certainly have amused him.

Reluctantly at daylight I got dressed and almost mechanically began to pack away some of the hated paraphernalia which had littered bathroom and bedroom for so long; I covered his wheelchair; I did not want these things surrounding him when he had to leave.

I had never experienced the practicalities of a death. My first thought was to telephone our doctor but of course it was still far too early. So, as I had so often done in recent years I turned to my dear and trusted neighbours the Clearys, and of all the kaleidoscope of memories of those first hours, the clearest is of Sally and Ross sitting with me at the table, composing lists, making gentle suggestions, and most specifically ensuring that I eat a bowl of cornflakes while they did so.

Then came the doctor – then the coroner, or was it the other way around – then Laura from the funeral home and her team. Leave me a minute with him, I asked, so they did. I was told later that there was quite a gathering at the front door to see him off in his ambulance.

Telephone calls to Jim and David. Poor, poor Jim, he could not have been more awkwardly placed to receive such news. He was away from his office in Lilongwe, the capital of Malawi, in the middle of some high level meetings; there were no direct flights until several days later. We agreed that I must go ahead with cremation and a memorial service in two days' time with David's help while Jim made his way as best he could; he joined us, grieving and weary, on December 12th – five days after talking to me.

"With David's help". David, flying from Toronto, was with me in the space of a few hours and for the next four days we navigated together this totally foreign, miserable, grief-laden system of Laying a Loved One to Rest. I cannot think how, in Jim's absence, I would have managed without him, or endured the presence of anyone else in his place. We sat around a table in the crematorium; we must have chosen a box, planned a service, we must have made many telephone calls , but I remember little of that. What I do remember vividly is our last visit to Vernon. The funeral home is out in the country so we drove awhile in the sunny cold December air. Mary by now was with us. In one of the many acts of kindness which supported us in these days, Joan Riding, her one-time minister from church and a long-time friend, had at my request picked Mary up from her home in Sandy Hill and delivered her to me.

At the Funeral Home, Laura greeted us with tea and cookies and then led us over to see Vernon. He lay in a very plain box on an equally plain kind of trestle; it could have been incongruous but for Vernon it seemed just fine, and David was pleased. Then David disappeared and I saw him walking up and down outside smoking a cigarette. Mary went back for another cookie.

On 10th December we had a short memorial gathering for Vernon in the Pinecrest Funeral chapel. I had not put its date in the newspaper obituary so the people present were just the few who I had telephoned; fifteen of our closest friends, plus two of his caregivers – and brother Bill. He had come from England the previous day. Driving from the airport in a red rented car – he stayed long enough to overlap with Jim, so by the end of the first week I had all the people who I needed most. David, the first to come was not only my strength and stay in the early hours and days, but because of an inescapable commitment at home he actually flew back to Toronto for 2 nights and then came back to

IT'S ODD, THE THINGS ONE REMEMBERS

Ottawa again. Truly we were all functioning on reserves we did not imagine we possessed.

Back to that memorial service. I have felt regret that I didn't give Vernon a more conventional farewell – more people, more words, above all more music. We lost out badly on that because David and I, having carefully chosen and put aside the CDs we wanted to play, discovered on arrival at the chapel that the discs were not there; their covers so hastily picked up were empty! I remembered then that Vernon had removed his favourite CDs into one bag to make it easier for himself to handle them, but it was too late to do anything but play the one available track provided by the crematorium. It was Onward Christian Soldiers!! He would have been horrified but of course we all belted it out. Bill read the usual Corinthians passage and also spoke, very well and plainly – none of his public persona there. Mary in her red dress stood up and told us all that she loved him, and would pray for him, "and all that". I chose some lines from the closing verse of Wordsworth's Ode on Intimations of Immortality (a formidable title for a beautiful poem). David spoke, not for long but so obviously from the bottom of his heart that I was moved closer to tears than by any other part of the short ceremony. And, the while, Vernon's ashes presided in his small cedarwood box with one single flower beside it. I carried him home and he stays with me still.

With Jim arrived, and David returned from his 48 hour Toronto turnaround, we organized a small gathering of DRB colleagues, condo residents and friends here at Westmount Place. This time it was Jim's turn to stand and speak for his father, and again make me deeply proud of Vernon's sons. As for those regrets about not giving him "a more conventional farewell", we all agreed that he would have been quite satisfied with these two gatherings. Except maybe for the lack of music!

One by one they had to leave. Bill took himself off to the airport in his bright red car, all his kindness, and advice and moments of fun, left to buoy me. I will never know what plans he had to change or cancel in order to stay a whole week with me, but he never said anything.

Then David left, with Jeff – David who had shared the whole novel experience with me from the start. And Jim; he stayed on awhile and we did a few things together. In particular I remember him taking me for a drive and gently persuading me that indeed there was no need to hurry home. Vernon wasn't waiting for care or cheer – I had *time* now, Jim said. When finally I left him at the airport – a quick embrace and he dancing off with his trolley full of huge bags – then I felt quite numb. I know what people mean when they say they are drained of emotion. Wouldn't want to stay that way for long but maybe for then it was some kind of anaesthetic at work.

My diary describes well the ups and downs of the ensuing days and weeks. Times busy with red tape, correspondence, loose ends; times equally busy with visits, visitors and outings in these new unaccustomed spaces of free time – I just could not get used to this – but all interspersed with the quiet, the sad, the mourning hours. I relived over and over our last days and I chided myself for not truly realizing how weary and discouraged Vernon must have been. I wondered if he was at peace now, he never having been the most peaceful of folk. But since I firmly believe that souls, if souls there are, return after death into the hearts of those who loved them, I decided that he was within me; that I could only hope that he knew that and was content.

With this new, unaccustomed gift of *time* – so difficult to realize that I possessed it – new avenues opened to me. People kept saying, you should travel now. At first I was in no hurry to do that, until I realized that would be exactly what Vernon would most want and expect me to do, he who was always so ready to up and go somewhere – preferably somewhere new. So in March 1999 Mary and I flew to Vancouver to visit her one-time counsellor and good friend Marria, then on by ferry to Victoria to stay with Sheila and Bill Chauvin. This was a couple linked to us by a series of coincidences. Some years before, I had worked for Bill in the Quality Assurance branch of the Defence Dept. (a very challenging and satisfying six months in a bilingual executive

IT'S ODD, THE THINGS ONE REMEMBERS

assistant position. At the end of it I was offered a permanent job by one of his colleagues which I had reluctantly to turn down – but that is a digression.) Learning that I had been on the Washington circuit, Mr. Chauvin asked if I knew Sheila Kinnear. Indeed I did, she having been a very busy and popular social convener at Canadian Joint Staff there – and a classy English lady to boot. Turned out that Sheila and Bill were then an item, pending his divorce; following that and his retirement they had moved to Victoria and we had kept in touch. So Mary and I discovered the pleasures of Spring on the British Columbia coast – magnolias and jasmine in Sheila's garden; masses of colourful flowerbeds in Stanley Park, "real" fish and chips on the waterfront. Returning to Ontario was a contrast indeed, but we were pleased with our adventure.

Over the next decade my travels continued. With Mary I took several coach tours in Canada and the USA; three flights with her to England, especially in May of 2000 when her 50th birthday was celebrated with a non-stop round of excitements involving uncle, aunt, cousins and friends. By myself I had the thrill of a visit to Malawi, thanks to Jacquie and Jim's kind encouragement and help. My only experience of Africa apart from previous short visits to Cairo and to Morocco with Vernon, and this still only a tiny piece of it, but for me important because I could finally share a small part of the expatriate life which had been theirs for all of Jim's working years and which now was coming to an end.

Zomba, Malawi, 1999 - visiting my grandchildren: with (l- to r) Michael, David, Jessie, and Jacquie

Further travels took me back to Cuba and Mexico, to Antigua in the West Indies, and to much of eastern Canada; Gaspesie, Prince Edward Island, the Maritime provinces and Newfoundland, as well as repeatedly to my well-loved Quebec. Most of these were with tour companies but none the worse for that – excellent value for money!

To my surprise but also great pleasure I had discovered a most amiable travel companion in Jim Irvine – his Prue had died the year before Vernon. We both were interested in keeping in touch with DRB and Radar group colleagues so it became logical to go to their functions together; there was the added common interest in Blue Sea Lake where two of Jim's daughters have properties. With time on our hands we began to plan some expeditions – made doubly attractive since the choice of destinations was left largely to me! Both being fairly easy-going people we had few arguments, enjoyed our explorations and our own company. Jim's willingness to let me be the leader and instigator gave me a new confidence in myself, and for his part he relished the lack of demands and what he called Peace and Quiet.

Certainly our families must have watched the development of this liaison with bemusement, if not alarm, but they were extremely

IT'S ODD, THE THINGS ONE REMEMBERS

tolerant and kind throughout; over the next several years we had many shared family celebrations. Sadly Jim's faculties began to fade and 14 years on he has no memory of those times, nor I believe of any other times, but I am deeply thankful that I received his particular support, and the new sense of myself which it gave me when I most needed it. And was able to reciprocate that support to him.

The rest of that last year of the 20th century brought inevitably a rising public excitement as we prepared to welcome the new one. Millennium events and ceremonies abounded; coins, souvenirs, publications, memoirs – "a century captured in photographs!" it was all very special and I wished Vernon had lived to see it. Jacquie, Jim and the grandchildren and I stood across Wellington Street from Parliament at midnight on December 31st and watched the minutes count down on the Peace Tower. What next? we wondered.

In fact from our family point of view it was a very big What Next because Jim's Malawi assignment was about to end; by the following summer they were tackling the huge challenge of settling permanently in Ottawa. Stuck in hotels, or at times with me in my flat; looking for a house, for schools, children feeling rootless and confused – and grandmother , still somewhat at sea in her own new widowed circumstances not being the support she should have been. Even after they had bought and settled in a pleasant, roomy home, for the first four years Jim still needed to commute from Washington, leaving Jacquie to handle all. Nevertheless, slowly and efficiently they worked through it all and established a secure home life .

Another "how I wish Vernon had lived to see…" happening was the arrival of Heidi Ritscher into our lives. David, still raw following Vernon's death, was working in the Royal Ontario Museum where he met a lady who had also lost her beloved father; this common bond led to other compatibilities, and to the joy of all our families Heidi and David joined forces and later married in 2001. We were a happy congregation in the chapel of Hart House at the University of Toronto. (But I never did get any of that delicious looking wedding cake – did anyone? And what happened to it?) Heidi being a Toronto native and David having lived and worked there for twenty years, they chose to stay and eventually, as Jacquie and Jim had done, created an attractive and welcoming home – a base for many delightful visits.

I often think how right for him are Vernon's daughters-in-law – if only he had known them both. Of course he and Jacquie were already good friends; they appreciated each others' forthright approach to life and could reciprocate without fear of offence. He and Heidi would surely have enjoyed the same mutual respect for definite opinions – for challenge and argument. Also, her family's Austrian roots and history would have interested him greatly. Instead it falls to me to appreciate and love them both on his behalf as well as my own – and how doubly blessed that makes me.

David and Heidi's wedding, 2001, with Heidi's mother Herta.

CHAPTER 11

AFTERWARDS

Family support or not, I had to shape my new life by myself and I began to do so. Buoyed all the way by Vernon's counsel – how surprised, and how humbled I was to discover that I had absorbed so much practical knowledge from him. From financial matters to car and home maintenance, thanks to his careful notes and records or to my own memories of his coaching, I began to "get my house in order". Significantly, I knew that I had enough money. With two thirds of his retirement pension plus my own OAP, CPP and a minute monthly offering from the British government in recognition of my short young working life in England; with careful, if conservative management of his investments; I was secure enough – provided I did not live too long. The apartment was fully paid for and I had no intention of leaving it. Mary is adequately supported for life by the provincial government and her inheritance, such as it may be, carefully protected by the terms of our Wills.

So, with this developing confidence in myself what did I do next? I bought a car! By myself, for myself I bought a mid-priced, mid-sized family Ford sedan – a conservative choice as most of our cars had been. But this one was a warm crimson red, and her name for reasons unknown became Josee. I remembered enough of Vernon's teaching that I could look after her basic needs; in time and after some expensive misjudgements I was able to tell the fellows at the garage that she didn't need *everything* doing that they suggested. She is now nearly 15 years old and though travelling less than in our first heady days together, still serves me well and I don't plan to part with her yet.

I expanded the time spent on existing interests and included one or two new ones. The former being my commitment to my friends in the OCAPDD programs and my support of the long-struggling national movement to legalise euthanasia and assisted suicide. This had begun as long ago as the 1970s when the first Senate debate on the subject took place and my (as well as many other peoples') correspondence was quite regularly published. Interestingly, when a few years ago I was talking to my ex WAAF friend Daphne on a visit to England she reminded me that I had in fact led a debate on that subject on one of our stations "and you gave an impassioned speech In Favour"! So that would be thirty years before 1970. I do not remember what first sparked my interest in so controversial a subject. It was fuelled, of course, in my early married days as I became familiar by circumstance, not by choice, with the institutions and hospitals filled with incurables such as my Johnnie. (Although the thrust of the argument now relates more to mercy at the *end* of life; there has long been a quiet rule of compassion among most doctors in cases like his).

New interests began with a gradual renewal of commitment to the Anglican Church – surprising to me, but it arose naturally enough at the time. Mary, wherever she lived, had always made a point of finding the nearest Anglican church and introducing herself there. Almost always she was made welcome, and over time and so many moves has created quite a chain of friends among various Ottawa congregations, including the present Dean of the Cathedral, several vicars and choir directors! After Vernon's death I began to go with her to her current parish church, which at that time was All Saints' Sandy Hill. A sturdy edifice of grey stone, with a squat tower, it stands at the corner of Laurier Avenue and Chapel Street directly opposite the one-time home of Sir Wilfrid Laurier. It is typical of many that were built in the middle of the nineteenth century by the proud citizens of Canada's new capital – lumbermen, stonemasons, merchants – Protestant and Catholic both, with large congregations and the guaranteed support of a solid rising middle class population. (Now, the social and demographic changes of a hundred years have greatly reduced those supporters and some of the churches have closed altogether, our dear All Saints among them.)

When going with Mary there I was so warmly welcomed, and found such an unexpected degree of comfort in the familiar rites and music, that I became for a few years a fairly active member. I joined the Altar Guild and was humbled to learn how much care and attention to accuracy is needed to correctly "dress" the church according to her calendar. To really burnish those heavy brass candlesticks and the huge heavy altar cross, to iron, oh so perfectly, the yards-long linen cloth for the communion table; to carefully unroll the different brocaded hangings and change them – purple for Easter, ruby red for Christmas; whites and golds … I began to see these not as mere ornamentation but as the symbols which they are: of dedication and faith . When at the close of the Maundy Thursday evening service the church is gradually darkened and the Guild silently strips the altar and chancel, bearing away the heavy brass, folding precisely the long table cloth (one person at each end, working inwards till they meet) until all is bare, the last dim light is extinguished and the congregation departs in silence – that is an experience I can only describe as sacred. Whatever 'sacred' means.

I also enjoyed reading the Lessons to the congregation, for which a bit of homework is essential if one is to make sense to one's listeners of some of the more obscure Bible passages – and by extension, to oneself. As with the Altar Guild work, I found myself thinking and learning more about ecclesiastical matters that, once my childhood interest in them faded, had for years been only a dim background to my life.

Nonetheless for all the solace and ease of the spirit which these rituals gave me I still could not – and cannot now – subscribe to the tenets of a true Christian belief. "I notice that you do not say the Creed" observed Robin Burns after attending a service at All Saints with me. I can't improve on the summary of my own "set of beliefs to live by" as I set them out earlier, in Chapter 2 of this memoir: "a mildly practical version of Christianity .... though rejecting the mythological aspects, yet I have drawn strength from my own interpretation of it".

Our connection with All Saints regrettably ended when Mary moved from her Sandy Hill apartment and came to live near me in the west end; it became more practical to join a local parish church close by. The people are just as welcoming and supportive, so eager to include us and share our interests and "problems" that my reserved northern nature sometimes cringes internally! but never could I show anything other than that same warm appreciation in return. I have read that in young countries like Canada and the United States the immigrant population looked to their churches as much for social and community support as for religious rituals. Although clearly the latter was and is integral and vital, yet I think some of that original function shapes congregations still, especially the rural, suburban ones and those with a younger base.

Often in the early days and months of bereavement one longs for some communication with the dead person – comforting as it is to talk to them, the conversation is one-sided. Once or twice I had a sense of Vernon being nearby, a faint echo as if he had spoken and then gone away. Then one day I found a tape that he had left for me. Tucked in among others on the shelf, wrapped loosely in a white envelope with just his name . I could not imagine what I was going to hear yet I seemed to know that it was for me, as indeed it was. A most clear and loving message, recorded one evening when I was out and he was, he said, coming to terms with the end of his life. To listen to it, to hear his voice so unexpectedly after months without it was the most moving experience I have ever had, a deep shock almost too much to bear. Then the frustration of not being able to reply, to thank him and say as I did out loud at the end:

"Why the hell couldn't you have said some of those things to me before?"

How sad that we mostly leave unsaid the words that we should, and say those that we should not. So how I treasure that little tape, even though I cannot reply to it.

IT'S ODD, THE THINGS ONE REMEMBERS

More happily, we had splendid celebrations of my 80th birthday in May 2004. Planned well ahead, they spread over several days. First with a gathering of family, friends and neighbours in our party room at Westmount Place, then with a picnic in Vincent Massey Park (this was probably the most fun, judging from the fact that my photo album has four pages devoted to that, against one for the first party), and in between a family dinner at Café Henri Burger across the river. Pat and Bill, Cecily and Bernhard, as well as all the Irvine family, for whom we were also celebrating five birthdays that week – I was indeed surrounded by fun and goodwill. And – truly the richest icing on an already rich cake – Jim had made a video from my photo albums; a mosaic of my life set to appropriate music! which he showed to the captive audience at the "formal" party. What a labour of love and how I treasure it.

After such a treat as that, most unexpected and astonishing was the surprise birthday celebration that he, Jacquie and the family gave me when I turned 85. I had spent the morning happily receiving phone calls, cards and flowers and we had already agreed on a family afternoon tea "but don't you do anything Mum, we will have it in the party room". So along they all came; Jacquie and Jim, Jessie, David, Michael and Mary, bearing more flowers, more loving greetings and the announcement that some were going down to the party room to "get things ready. We will let you know when you can come". Michael and I went to the kitchen to arrange the flowers; Mary, sitting in the living room, got up when the clock struck three and said she was going down now. In retrospect I remember Michael giving her a nod – OK – as also, in retrospect, I remember him hastily texting a message into his phone when I, some minutes later, suggested that he and I go too.

He opened the door of the party room and I stepped in, but barely two steps before I fell back against the wall in total stupefaction. The room was decorated with balloons and banners, the big table laden with food and drink and a very large cake, *and it was absolutely packed with people*. Many of my dearest friends, condominium neighbours, ex-neighbours and my family – I never did count how many but they were all there smiling at me, laughing at my obvious astonishment, all dressed up and so lovely and there was I in slacks and an old sweater. Around the room I went, greeting but half-believing as I came by one dear face after another – how could they all be here, together, just like that? The answer must be, by a degree of organization worthy of a campaign, and I know that my Jim was at the heart of it even if he enlisted help with names and telephone numbers as he must have done. All I really remember doing is constantly apologizing for "being in old clothes". Of course nobody cared, but I did. Why didn't I go and change – it never occurred to me. Truly I was mostly in a state of unbelieving, that all this effort had been expended for me.

Other milestone birthdays were well celebrated in the course of these last two decades. Jacquie and Jim turned 60 in 2012 and family and friends came from all over the world; on their Gatineau cottage flagpole the ensigns of different countries changed daily for over a week. There were gatherings there and at their home, there was an evening cruise on the Ottawa River which gave an opportunity to show off our fine city by moonlight – it was justly praised. An event which had taken a huge amount of planning and effort by the birthday people themselves – I think they found it worthwhile. Certainly it gave a great many people a chance to show their love and admiration for Jacquie and Jim.

Forward to 2014 (chronology goes by the board in this narration) when to mark my 90th birthday I chose, instead of yet another party, to take my children to England for a week. This more accurately translates to Jim and David taking Mary and me. It was an undertaking, yes, once I had committed to it I felt guilty realizing how much effort and time would be required from my sons – and from Pat and Bill who had to face this invasion. But thanks to them all we did indeed go, and come back again, without incident, illness or injury (all of which I had envisaged as likely). Mary of course accepted all as her due and became an experienced, if grumpy air traveler: "if they want to see my boarding pass and passport so often why don't we just give it to them and stay in England?"

IT'S ODD, THE THINGS ONE REMEMBERS

David, Mary, and Jim – Oxford pub; 90th birthday trip to England.

How many times did I hear Happy Birthday sung that May month, in surely a dozen different places by so many different people – until the very last one, called cheerily by Jim as he waved the three of us off at Glasgow airport and went to meet Jacquie (who was arriving for a trip with Jim to Scotland) – as we left?

"Happy Birthday Mum!"

Many times indeed, but never so many as I need to thank my dear family for making it so.

On 9th May 2010 Mary held her 60th birthday party here in Westmount Place. She had anticipated it for a very long time and done most of the planning herself, including the guest list. In fact the final production rather overwhelmed her; the many greetings and hugs, the presents and the photos – so many requests to "smile, Mary!" produced eventually some rather bemused expressions instead. Withal, it was a happy success. Guests departed, family scattered. David the younger flying back to the University of Waterloo. (He had come specially for the occasion being the only available sibling. Jessie was in Australia and Michael at UBC had just begun a summer research project.) Jim, Jacquie, David and Heidi went home to Wood Avenue and Mary and I, cheerfully exhausted, upstairs to bed.

173

Late that same evening Jacquie and Jim were awakened by a knock at the door from police officers come to tell them that Michael had drowned that afternoon. He had run in a marathon and then gone for a swim in the sea to cool off. He dove into the water and didn't come up again.

I feel almost presumptuous to write of Michael's death here in what is supposed to be a chronicle of my own life. Even though I am his loving grandmother yet his story belongs to those closest to him; the right to tell it is theirs. His loss was by far the greatest tragedy to have befallen any of us ; the shock and anguish deeper than anything we had experienced. While Jacquie and Jim, Jessie and David closed in together for their own survival the rest of us – Mary and I, David and Heidi, the Australia family, a multitude of friends literally all over the world – we stood by with our hearts aching, but all needing to deal with the practicalities which now swamped us.

Jessie flew home. She had been about to begin a long-planned trip across Australia. David, barely back at university after Mary's party, sleepless, turned round and flew home again. The four of them went together to Vancouver to bring Michael home. There they held a memorial service, met his friends and professors, saw his rooms and the work he had so eagerly begun on the research project which was to occupy him the next few months. (In an email not long before, he had proudly told me about the grant he had received for it – "so I'm sorry I won't be back in Ottawa this summer. But I'll be home for Christmas!")

Within the week they were all back. Another memorial service; oh so many, many friends did Michael have, and they spoke of him, as did his teachers, as did his father, and his Uncle David sang for him. In the garden at his home prayer flags were strung through the trees, they are there still four years later. In Beechwood Cemetery a strong young tree grows over Michael's name.

How did his family bear all this in so short a space of time I cannot know; grief seems to generate strength. Life doesn't stand still for death; of course everybody "carried on". For David it was essential to return to school even with his weight of loneliness. Jessie, thankfully, stayed

IT'S ODD, THE THINGS ONE REMEMBERS

with her parents for several months to support them, and her being there certainly gave me comfort.

Summing up a great deal that I wrote at that time I said:

My husband is dead
My son is dead
My grandson is dead
And I am left with a daffy daughter at 86 years old.
If that isn't a topsy-turvy world, what is?

I also said, Nothing will ever be the same, and of course it has not been and will not be. Jacquie and Jim survived by restlessness, it seemed to me; for the next year or so they were constantly off somewhere, or to the Quebec lake which is the refuge for all of them. On Michael's birthday that December we all sat round the fire with tea and looked at photo albums.

Jessie and David both graduated successfully and have managed to find and hold good jobs at a time when many of their contemporaries do not. They have become – by any standards not just proud grandmother's – mature, gifted and exceptional people. Michael would have been doing that by now, wouldn't he?

> "A death so unforeseen that our sense of the ordinary
> died with him.
> The normal grasses of life never quite grew back".
>
> Elizabeth Hay.

Four years have passed now since Michael died. We the family are all healthy and occupied; sometimes we are happy and sometimes we are sad, and always, always, Michael is with us and makes sure that we live our lives on, even if none of us can ever quite match his richness of spirit and talent, his zest and thirst for experience and knowledge, the abundant embrace of life which he held all his nineteen years.

NINA ANN SMITH

with Michael, 2009

RUST-SMITH, Michael
It is with the greatest sadness in the world that we announce the accidental death of Michael Rust-Smith, beloved son of Jacquie Rust and Jim Smith, and brother to Jessie and David. Michael lived a full, interesting, and joyous life. He had an endless curiosity about the natural world, and a boundless love of life. He was an artist, a scientist, a dancer, a pirate, and a ninja. He sought truth in all things, and touched countless lives with his love and enthusiasm. Michael died in Vancouver on Sunday, May 9 while swimming after a 10 k. run. He was 19 years old. He is survived by his grandmother Ann and aunt Mary (Ottawa) grandmother Cecily, uncles Tim, Chris, and David, aunts Fiona and Verena, and cousins Sally and Jack (Melbourne, Australia), and uncle David and aunt Heidi (Toronto). Our hearts are broken, but he would want us only to remember the great joy that was his life. A celebration of Michael's life for his friends in Ottawa will be held at the Unitarian Church, 30 Cleary Ave at 5:30 p.m. Monday, May 17, followed by a reception at our home.

IT'S ODD, THE THINGS ONE REMEMBERS

As for me; now I am ninety years old so have graduated from Old Age into Very Old Age. I was becoming accustomed to the former state but it is hard to come to terms with the new one. I pretend that nothing has changed but have to admit that yes, there are new challenges. I feel – different. Physically I am very well and very lucky. I exercise and walk every day, I take – to the amazement of my contemporaries – only one prescription medicine. But I wish my brain functioned as well as my body. I know that I should have better developed media skills; that I should expand the use of my cellphone beyond keeping it in my purse, "just in case" but usually turned off. Music and reading are as important as always but my books are still the paper kind and music comes from CDs and the radio. Truly I realize that I am falling behind in the wired world; I am very aware for instance that most family communication takes place on more sophisticated devices than I possess; that being only reluctantly on Facebook – not Twittering – puts me out of touch not only with them but with most of the population under eighty years old. Nevertheless, lazy or uninclined, I convince myself that I can learn what I need by my own ancient methods.

In any case, as we both grow older I spend more time with or on behalf of Mary. In theory this should not be so. Her placement in a bright, spacious apartment within walking distance of my home, with round-the-clock staff and Jim's increasing support and care for her were supposed to ease me, her aging parent, out of the picture. However since I am clearly still mobile, still drive a car, and live across the road, it is naturally difficult for Mary to see any reason why I should not be as available as I have ever been. And equally difficult for me to pretend otherwise. She spends alternate weekends with me, we attend the same church, I board her beloved cat and give house room to many of her possessions. How can I then assume to be unavailable? So we continue to be seen as Ann-and-Mary (quite recently I was greeted by a woman who said apologetically "I didn't recognize you without your daughter"!) and it seems that only a dramatic change in my own circumstances – illness, or a move away, would change that.

Just sometimes – but rarely, because it is a road not walkable without darkness – I imagine how hugely different our family life would be had Johnnie and Mary been born whole. There would be great-grandchildren no doubt! – and a daughter to take me places instead of the other way round (if she were not, as well she might be, living at the other side of the world). Anyway there is no need to go that road, being blessed as I am with all the support I could ask for from the family I do have; the family which I cherish every day.

Mary and I also continued to visit our beloved Blue Sea Lake. Its attraction was as strong as ever and to write of it releases so many memories that it should before now have had a passage of its own. Here, belatedly:

There are of course many attractive "lake properties" closer to Ottawa, and when we first came to live here many friends and colleagues invited us to look at theirs. But we had enjoyed our explorations of the Laurentian area while living in Quebec, and now had only to cross the Ottawa River to be once again in that Province; to find similar ranges of low hills, rolling farmland and villages; following the beautiful Gatineau valley north to more forested, quieter country.

Blue Sea (you soon learn to omit the superfluous word "lake") lies about 90 kilometres north of Ottawa and west of the highway between the small towns of Gracefield and Maniwaki. Until the middle of the 20th century there was a regular rail service; the train ran all the way up from Gatineau (then called Hull) with random stops as needed to drop off families who, with their considerable luggage, were establishing themselves in their summer homes. A neighbour of mine whose family owned an island in Blue Sea tells of such an annual rite. The train actually halted at a spot where the line ran close to the shore. Two boats were waiting; adults, children, pets, and possessions were transferred safely and rowed away; the train continued on its journey. How much more fun that would have been than bumping along a dusty and pot-holed lane with a loaded car after a long hot trek up the busy weekend highway!

IT'S ODD, THE THINGS ONE REMEMBERS

I have often walked along that now deserted track – and had some good fishing – at the very spot where the train unloaded the Sherwood family so many years ago.

We never owned a cottage, preferring to keep our summers flexible to include other travels if needed, but over the years we rented a variety of places on stretches of that lovely shore. At first we would sometimes go up for weekends as well as for longer holidays. If the weather forecast was good I would telephone Madame Aline Lacroix on a Friday evening. Who gave me her name? I forget, but she owned a number of properties around the tiny village of Blue Sea which circles the southern end of the lake.. Oui, Mme. Smith! she had a "chalet" available for 2 nights; come, and she would show it to us. $7.00 per night was the rate! We never quite knew what to expect; there could be an indoor toilet or not, there could be a cooking stove or not; it might or not be on the shore. But always clean and fun, and always a rowboat available from her nephew Ray. Among other enterprises he ran the gas station across the road from the lake, always our first stop on arrival in the village to catch up on the latest news. Sixty years later he remains a loyal ami.

Blue Sea Lake

Gradually the rentals became scarce as people bought, renovated and settled in the properties. Mme Aline retired and died peacefully in her late 90s. But Ray continued to find places for us as we requested, though less often as children grew and lives became busier. Vernon and the boys had become good water-skiers and sometimes friends were invited to share. "They are welcome if they contribute to the cost of the gas for the boat" was Vernon's caveat at those times!

The family dispersed; Vernon died; always Blue Sea remained a refuge. Eventually it was up to Mary and me to keep the memories alive, and we did so most happily , with Ray's help , for many more years. On my desk as I write is the photo of a small cottage which Mary and I retreated to in the later times, but which has been demolished since in the name of "progress". We called it our cottage, and so it remains in my memory.

Thanks to goddaughter Susan Irvine, her sister Elizabeth, their families, and their lovely properties there, I am still able to visit Blue Sea ; it is with me still. I have stipulated that after my death my ashes be scattered on its deep waters. Since both Vernon and Mary have requested that theirs be taken to England, this appears to be a significant if subconscious symbol of my own commitment – and thanks – to Canada. Yes?

I spoke of moving out of the apartment. Visiting as I do now so many friends in retirement homes, I for a time contemplated following them. Serious consideration; tours of handsome buildings, cosy rooms, "entertainment", meals prepared by someone else, companionship – all of course costing many many dollars.... After consultation with the Js and Heidi and David , and doing some rough arithmetic, I decided no, not just yet. But I know it has to come, if only to force me to drastically strip away all that I do not need and to train myself for the simpler domestic life I will have to lead when infirmity and illness do catch up with me.

Meanwhile I stay here, in my too-big flat with too many books and pictures, far too many plates and cups and saucers and too much

IT'S ODD, THE THINGS ONE REMEMBERS

furniture. But with a balcony where I love to sit on summer evenings with a drink, the cat and my flowers. Where I can still glimpse just a small stretch of the river which hasn't yet been obscured by the burgeoning trees. (Never having lived so long in one place I did not until now appreciate the fact that trees actually grow!) And where the sunsets over the water and the line of hills beyond are beautiful, and when storm clouds gather there the rain with the sunset brings rainbows. A huge solace and refuge is my balcony. I doubt there will be one with my room in the Old Folks' Home and almost certainly it will not have this view.

And how long will I stay in this comfortable, expensive old folks' home when I do get there? That is the question mark which cannot be erased. To paraphrase Woody Allen, I am not afraid to die but I don't like the idea of dying. I am thankful that I was not raised with any belief in a life after death. (Though Theo and I were very taken with the theory of reincarnation and read a great deal on the subject. He was convinced that we had known each other in a previous life, though he didn't say in what form.) I would like the opportunity to talk to Vernon, I would have so much to tell him. And also to my mother; I would like them both to know how well I have managed on my own. But then I do talk to them and listen to them, all the time; much counsel do I receive from both if I carefully listen. So I'll be satisfied with that.

If I am lucky I may be able to die, as one or two of my friends have done, "at a time and in a manner of my own choosing". If as is more likely I shall be at the mercy of other peoples' care, I hope that by that time the concept of merciful assisted death, which I have supported in writing, vocally, and financially for over thirty years, will have become a legal option, making everything so much easier for all concerned.

An autobiography is supposed to end with some well-crafted words on the nature of Life and of Death – some profound summary of one's past and speculation on one's future. Looking for inspiration on this I have just re-read the ending of my mother's semi-fictional autobiography "Portrait of Julie". Her writing is much superior to mine, as was her intellect and her grasp of the human condition, and her philosophy was coloured by strong religious and spiritual beliefs which I do not hold. However, the theme of her final paragraph is contained thus:

> "One thing I have learned is to recognise, without seeking to understand, the mystery of the many facets of human love."

So, tied to that sentiment, perhaps the simplest way to end this story – this very amateur account of ninety years in the life of one very average product of middle-class Britain in the twentieth century – is to quote some lines which came to me completely spontaneously as I sat on that balcony some years ago. I wrote them down in shorthand in about three minutes; I was sober, untroubled and not thinking of anything in particular. It was as though they came out of my head from nowhere. Clearly they must have "wanted out".

> "Is this what it all boils down to? An old woman sitting in her eyrie, gazing across her balcony flowers to the river, woods and hills. A lifetime telescoped to a few quiet moments of remembering the girl from Kent who bounced through her secure and happy beginnings, though without much imagination or forethought – so she carried on into all that the future threw at her, stage by surprising stage. And met each one, endured or adapted but still kept a core of optimism and innate pleasure in new things, which enabled her not only to survive but find islands of quieter satisfaction – even, from time to time – joy.

IT'S ODD, THE THINGS ONE REMEMBERS

It has been a life in which love appeared in many forms. And where love is, the spirit is indestructible.

Maybe that is the Holy Ghost in us!"

N. Ann Smith

Ottawa
October 2014

EPILOGUE

The writing of a life story is supposedly a tidying up, a tying of the loose ends into a neat package. Followed, if one is fortunate, by a year or two of quiet reflection.

When in October 2014 I noted in my diary that this manuscript was finished I wrote firmly "– and I swear that I will not add one word to it."

Two years on I find myself, not in that promised time of peaceful winding down but faced with a dark and dreadful challenge for which nothing in my long experience has prepared me; my Mary's diagnosis of Amyotrophic Lateral Sclerosis - ALS.

How long will she live? Will I outlive her? And if I do, will I be strong enough to help and succour her? We are in a race to the finish you and I, my beloved daughter.

For now we all share the weight. Jim is my rock and Mary's unfailing first port of call. He and Jacquie are omnipresent for us; more practical, more wide awake than I. David and Heidi the same, frustrated by distance but always there. No matter who wins this slow race, Mary or I, the burden will land on their shoulders – my no-longer-young children.

Unfair! Of course it's grossly, bloody unfair, and don't dare to tell me that Life Is Never Fair and that God Never Promised You a Rose Garden. Brave, stoical Mary, who has managed the many limitations of her damaged body and mind for 65 years and had so proudly achieved her version of "independence", only to be unable now to eat or speak, besieged by a host of bewildering frustrations and discomforts.

Loss of speech! She was five years old before she could talk, but then she talked and sang her way through; one-armed and lame, with all those faulty neurons rolling around in the damaged half of her brain; Mary made her life.

She makes it still, through the fog of the wicked illness, denying her tiredness and smiling as she writes for me on her Boogie Board. I write this on the eve of her 66th birthday, which of course will be grandly celebrated as she has always insisted it be; "please be sure to bring my blue and white dress over on Monday".

My heart breaks each day and I do not know where I am being led.

May 2016 _____

14th September 2018

Mary died in the early hours of this morning.

So she "won" the race between us and I must carry on to the finishing post without her.

May the rest of the course be short.

NAMES AND DATES

Name	Born/Died	Year
Family in Part I		
Norman Priestley Bentley	born Lancaster died Sutton Valence, Kent	1899 1969
Ellen Banks Bentley	born Rosedale, Yorkshire died Temple Sowerby, Cumbria	1896 1984
Nina Ann Bentley	born Sutton Valence, Kent	1924
Fredric William "Bill" Priestley Bentley	born Sutton Valence, Kent	1932
Adéle Patricia "Pat" Bentley née Berry	born Cockermouth, Cumbria	1936
James Smith	born Blackburn, Lancashire died Sidmouth, Devon	1892 1956
Lilian Smith née Drake	born Birmingham died Sidmouth, Devon	1896 1969
Vernon Smith	born Birmingham died Ottawa, Canada	1920 1998
John David Vernon Smith	born Enfield, Middlesex died South Ockendon, Essex	1948 1953
Family in Part II		
Anna Mary Smith	born Enfield, Middlesex died Ottawa	1950 2018
William James Smith	born Aldenham, Hertfordshire	1952
David Mark Smith	born Hamilton, Ontario	1956
Jacqueline Renata Rust	born Melbourne, Australia	1952
Heidi Herta Ritscher	born Toronto, Ontario	1967
Jessica Ann Rust-Smith	born Washington D.C.	1986
David Christopher Rust-Smith	born Washington D.C.	1988
Michael Timothy James Rust-Smith	born Washington D.C. died Vancouver, B.C.	1990 2010

ACKNOWLEDGEMENTS

An autobiography, by definition, is written by one person, but it needs some very brave helpers to bring it to life.

This small one would still be gathering dust on the shelf where I stashed it five years ago, had my elder son, Jim Smith, not encouraged and helped me to resurrect it. From his first detailed and sensitive suggestions, corrections and clarifications, neatly encapsulated in the margins of the manuscript; to patiently steering me through scores of photographs, either resurrected from musty albums or magically appearing on my computer screen and helping me position them; Jim's commitment and encouragement have kept me going.

And those photographs would not "appear magically" if my younger son, David, had not over the last several years spent many hours sorting, assembling and transposing the slides, prints and videos that have recorded my own life and that of our family. To my untrained eyes the resultant record is an instant marvel, but I sense how much care and skill David has committed to it. Apart from a few from my childhood, most of them were taken by Vernon my husband over a period of fifty years; a meticulous record which I am only now fully appreciating for the care and affection with which it was created.

So – my most loving thanks to the men in my life.

The bravest of the "brave helpers" is without doubt my scribe/ copy-editor/ computer whiz/ endlessly patient tutor/ dear friend/ and great-goddaughter, Maryanna Guillet. When she agreed to "the job", sight unseen, she did not know how many cold winter trips she would have to make from her home several miles away (chauffeured by my equally dear friend and goddaughter, her super-mum, Susan.) Nor that she would spend much extra time untangling the web of errors and piles of Word documents which her computer-illiterate employer had created. With patience, humour and with truly remarkable technical skill, Maryanna brought this manuscript to life. She must know how grateful and impressed I am by her commitment. Luvya, girl!

Finally, a special thanks to Liza Weppenaar at FriesenPress, without whose invaluable help and guidance this book would never have come into being.

ABOUT THE AUTHOR

Nina Ann Smith (Bentley) was born in Sutton Valence, in Kent, in 1924. She served as a Radar Operator in the WAAF during World War II. Like thousands of women of her generation, she crossed the Atlantic after the war in search of a new life, an odyssey that led her to Canada, Washington, and Mexico. The mother of two disabled children, she has been active for over 60 years in championing services for the developmentally disabled.

Ann Smith now lives in Ottawa, Canada. Although she has written throughout her life, this is her first book.